D0866400

McCulloch v. Maryland:

STATE V. FEDERAL POWER

SUPREME COURT MILESTONES

McCulloch v. Maryland:

STATE V. FEDERAL POWER

SUSAN DUDLEY GOLD

PAUL VI H.S. LIBRARY
10675 FAIRFAX BLVD.
FAIRFAX, VA 22030

 **Marshall Cavendish**
Benchmark
New York

Marshall Cavendish Benchmark
99 White Plains Road
Tarrytown, NY 10591
www.marshallcavendish.us

Copyright © 2008 by Susan Dudley Gold

All rights reserved. No part of this book may be reproduced or utilized in any form or
by any means electronic or mechanical including photocopying, recording, or by any
information storage and retrieval system, without permission from the copyright
holders.

All Internet sites were available and accurate and available when sent to press.

Library of Congress Cataloging-in-Publication Data

Gold, Susan Dudley.
McCulloch v. Maryland : state v. federal power / by Susan Dudley Gold.
p. cm. — (Supreme Court milestones)
Includes bibliographical references and index.
ISBN 978-0-7614-2587-8
1. McCulloch, James W.—Trials, litigation, etc. 2. Bank of the United
States (Baltimore, Md.)—Trials, litigation, etc. 3. Maryland—Trials,
litigation, etc. 4. Banks and banking, Central—Law and legislation—United
States—History. 5. Exclusive and concurrent legislative powers—United
States—History. 6. State rights—History. I. Title. II. Title: McCulloch
versus Maryland. III. Series.
KF228.M318G65 2007
346.73'0821223—dc22
2007000581

Photo research by Connie Gardner

Cover photo by The Granger Collection

The photographs in this book are used by permission and courtesy of: *The Granger
Collection:* 2, 3, 98-99, 109, 114, 124, 136; *Art Resource:* The New York Public Library,
6; Reunion des Musees Nationaux, 32; National Portrait Gallery, Smithsonian Institu-
tion, 53; *NorthWind Picture Archive:* 10, 13, 16, 30, 40, 42, 94, 107; *Getty Images:* Hulton
Archive, 15, 62, 71, 84,88; *Corbis:* Bettmann, 22-23, 26; Oscar White, 104; Jason
Reed/Reuters, 112.

Publisher: Michelle Bisson
Art Director: Anahid Hamparian
Series Designer: Sonia Chaghatzbanian

Printed in China
1 3 5 6 4 2

contents

The First National Bank in Philadelphia. The landmark U.S. Supreme Court case *McCulloch* v. *Maryland* established the right of the federal government to create a national bank as part of its duties. More importantly, the case upheld the supremacy of the federal government over the individual states and set the course of the U.S. government.

Introduction

THE HEROES OF THE AMERICAN REVOLUTION freed the colonies from British control; the framers of the Constitution set up our government "of the people, by the people, for the people." But it was the early U.S. Supreme Court, under the leadership of Chief Justice John Marshall, that established the United States as a nation. Until the Court's rulings in several landmark cases, including *McCulloch* v. *Maryland*, the union was less a nation than a confederation of sovereign states.

In 1819 a Maryland bank manager's actions triggered a showdown between the federal and state governments and led to the Supreme Court decision that changed the course of the nation's history. James McCulloch, who managed the Baltimore branch of the Bank of the United States, refused to pay the $15,000 tax the state of Maryland had levied on the bank's currency. That tax applied only to banks chartered outside the state. The branch, part of the federal bank established by Congress in 1816, claimed it was exempt from state taxes. Maryland took McCulloch to court, and the case worked its way through the legal system to the Supreme Court.

The case involved much more than a bank tax. It pitted the federal government—just three decades old—against the venerable power of the individual states. Both sides claimed supremacy over the other. Federalists and nationalists believed that Maryland's actions threatened the existence of the young democracy. As merely a compact between the states with no overriding control, the nation, they contended, would not survive.

States' rights proponents viewed the federal bank as an example of Congress's attempts to usurp their power. They feared a return to conditions before the Revolution and believed that the bank was the first step in subjugating states under a despotic, out-of-control central government.

Congress incorporated the bank as a way to help stabilize the wildly fluctuating national economy. The government claimed Congress had the power to create the bank—and set up branches in the states—as part of its financial responsibilities to the nation. Among other things, the Constitution gave Congress the power to impose and collect taxes, borrow money, regulate commerce, and coin money—all of which Congress hoped a federal bank could help accomplish. In addition the Constitution stated that Congress had the power "to make all laws which shall be necessary and proper for carrying into execution the foregoing powers." The government took the position that the bank was a "necessary and proper" way to carry out its financial goals. By taxing federal currency, the bank claimed, the state of Maryland was interfering with Congress's goals and should be stopped.

Maryland contended that it controlled corporations within its borders and had a constitutional right to tax them. The state portrayed the Constitution and the national government it created as a compact among the individual states. Maryland's advocates claimed that the national government derived its powers from the states, but the states themselves retained supreme power over their territory and the people and entities within. These supporters of states' rights relied on the Constitution, too. The Tenth

Amendment, part of the Bill of Rights, set aside for the states (and the people) all powers not specifically granted to Congress: "The powers not delegated to the United States by the Constitution, nor prohibited by it to the States, are reserved to the States respectively, or to the people." Furthermore, they noted, the Constitution barred the state from taxing imports and exports; it said nothing about federal banks.

The Supreme Court's resolution of the dispute would set the course of American history. Declaring that the American people "did not design to make their government dependent on the States," Chief Justice John Marshall, in an opinion supported by a unanimous Court, upheld the principle of national supremacy. By doing so, the Court acknowledged the legitimacy of the national government and empowered it to operate as an independent entity whose laws took precedence over those of the individual states.

The decision also opened up interpretation of the Constitution to include "implied powers," giving Congress the power to undertake actions not specifically listed in the Constitution as long as the means served a constitutional end. In the years following the decision, the principle of national supremacy would be tested severely, challenged by the Civil War in the 1860s, by white supremacists in the twentieth century, and by states' rights advocates today. It has survived for more than two centuries, built upon the *McCulloch* decision—"the cornerstone of the subsequent constitutional development of the nation," in the words of Supreme Court Justice Robert Jackson—and incorporated in a Constitution "intended to endure for ages to come."

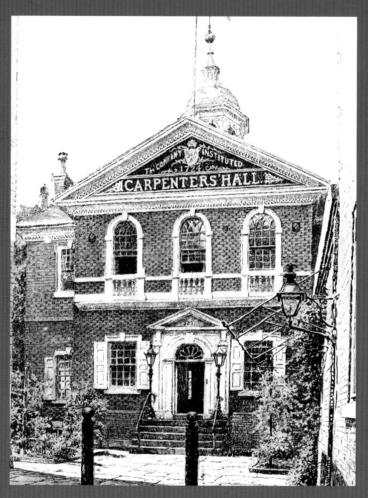

Early American leaders held the First Congressional Congress in 1774 at Carpenter's Hall in Philadelphia.

one
CONFEDERATION V. UNION

OUTRAGE OVER TAXES BRITAIN IMPOSED on the colonies led Americans to hold the First Continental Congress in September and October of 1774. Representatives from twelve colonies forged a compact agreeing to boycott British goods. Designed to convince King George III to lift the onerous taxes, the Articles of Association instead helped spark the growing protests that eventually led to the American Revolution.

When the compact failed to sway the British, the Second Continental Congress met on May 10, 1775. By then the first battles of the American Revolution had already been fought at Lexington and Concord, Massachusetts. The main focus of the delegates became the management of the war, including the creation of an army. Georgia, the last of the original thirteen colonies to support the Congress, finally agreed to send delegates, who joined the gathering on July 20.

On July 4, 1776, the American colonists issued the Declaration of Independence, proclaiming their determination to be free of British rule. Only their resolve to wage a war to separate themselves from Britain united the thirteen colonies, however. Little else held the separate colonies together. Even in the midst of war, the colonies disagreed on the form of government they should adopt. After almost a year of heated debate, the Continental

Congress finally agreed on a compromise measure that formed a national government but allowed the colonies to retain most of their individual rights. Passed on November 15, 1777, the Articles of Confederation and Perpetual Union bound the colonies together in a loose confederation to be known as the United States of America. The document established one national legislative body, the U.S. Congress, which oversaw foreign relations and had the power to declare war. Under the pact, the states retained sovereignty and continued to operate in most areas as independent entities.

A confederation of sovereign states

The Articles of Confederation required adoption by all thirteen colonies before going into effect. Leaders of the Continental Congress, noting that Americans needed to remain united in their fight for freedom, urged the colonies to ratify the Articles of Confederation quickly. In a letter to the states, the Congress acknowledged "the difficulty of combining in one general system the various sentiments and interests of a continent divided into so many sovereign and independent communities." Despite these differences, however, Congress called upon the colonies to ratify the Articles of Confederation "under a conviction of the absolute necessity of uniting all our councils and all our strength, to maintain and defend our common liberties."

South Carolina led the way, ratifying the document less than three months later, on February 5, 1778. Other states followed grudgingly, some taking years to debate the issue. The Articles of Confederation at last became effective on March 1, 1781, when the final state, Maryland, ratified the document. Maryland delayed its approval until a dispute over land ownership could be settled.

Under the new confederation, each state had one vote; the state legislature was responsible for appointing

D URING THE A MERICAN R EVOLUTION, THE COLONISTS PRINTED C ONTINEN -
TAL BILLS LIKE THE ONES ILLUSTRATED IN THIS WOODCUT.

delegates to Congress. Although Congress could declare war, it had no power to force the states to comply with requests for soldiers or money to pay war expenses. That created problems for a nation in the midst of battle. Only days before the end of the American Revolution, army officers threatened to overpower Congress, by force if necessary, to obtain pay and other benefits promised but not yet delivered by the government. On March 15, 1783, General George Washington met with the men and convinced them not to take action. "Let me conjure you," Washington exhorted his men, "in the name of our common country, as you value your own sacred honor, as you respect the rights of humanity, and as you regard the military and national character of America, to express your utmost horror and detestation of the man who wishes, under any specious pretenses, to overturn the liberties of our country, and who wickedly attempts to open the floodgates of civil discord and deluge our rising empire in blood."

Washington's eloquence averted that crisis, but the weak federal government would continue to pose major obstacles for the new nation. On April 11, 1783, Congress officially proclaimed the war over and reaffirmed the independence of the United States of America. Almost immediately, the states began to assert their separate interests. No longer united by the war, they pulled in many different directions. Under the Articles of Confederation, the national government had no power to do anything not specifically mentioned in the document. The federal government could not enforce laws, levy taxes, or perform other duties without first obtaining the approval of all thirteen states. That turned out to be nearly impossible to do, since each state's priorities differed from those of the others and state leaders put their region's concerns ahead of national interests. In fact, the name of the new nation

BANK

appearing to be the disposition of the Gentlemen in this City to establish a BANK on liberal inciples, the stock to consist of specie only, they therefore hereby invited to meet To-Morrow ening at Six o'Clock, at the Merchants Coffee House ere a plan will be submitted to their consideration

from New York Packet
February 23, 1784

AN EARLY NEWSPAPER RAN THIS NOTICE INVITING CITY LEADERS TO A MEETING TO DISCUSS THE FORMATION OF A BANK IN NEW YORK. THE MEETING EVENTU-ALLY LED TO THE FOUNDING OF THE BANK OF NEW YORK. ALEXANDER HAMILTON, AT THE TIME A PROMINENT NEW YORK LAWYER, WROTE THE BANK'S CONSTITUTION AND SPEARHEADED THE EFFORT TO ESTABLISH THE STATE BANK.

itself reflected the diverse makeup of the country. People referred to *these* United States, treating it not as a single entity but as a collection of loosely bound states.

Besieged by complaints from individual states threat-ening to withdraw from the fragile confederation, the founders knew they would have to "form a more perfect union." They also knew, however, that their fellow Ameri-cans, cherishing their newfound freedom from a powerful king, would not easily or willingly turn over control to a strong federal government. It became apparent to many of the new nation's leaders that to survive the United States would have to establish a strong federal government.

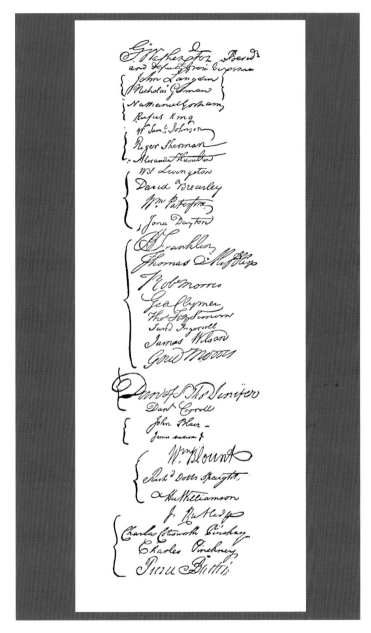

SIGNATURES OF THE LEADERS OF THE CONSTITUTIONAL CONVENTION, HELD IN 1787, AT WHICH THE U.S. CONSTITUTION WAS DRAFTED.

Federalists v. Antifederalists

Those who believed in a strong central government became known as Federalists. Most were landowners and businessmen who supported the national government's efforts to aid industry and encourage commerce. They had their strongest support in New England and sections of the middle states. Alexander Hamilton, a leader in the Federalist movement, and others began urging states to hold a new convention to craft a constitution that would strengthen Congress and give more power to the federal government. "It has ever been my opinion," Hamilton wrote his friend and fellow Federalist Robert Morris around 1783, "that Congress ought to have complete sovereignty in all but the mere municipal law of each state; and I wish to see a convention of all the States, with full power to alter and amend finally and irrevocably the present futile and senseless confederation." At this same time, Hamilton began lobbying for a national bank, as well as a federal army.

In 1787 fifty-five delegates from the thirteen former colonies met in Philadelphia for a Constitutional Convention. After four months of heated debate, the delegates drew up a written constitution, listing the rights and responsibilities of every citizen and dividing power between the states and a central government. The novel document these founders produced became the U.S. Constitution, today the world's oldest written constitution.

Thus began a bitter battle between the Federalists and other supporters of the Constitution and their opponents, the antifederalists, as they were called. Led by James Monroe and Patrick Henry, among others, the antifederalists opposed the adoption of the Constitution and its strong national government. They favored a more informal compact that would allow the individual states to retain their power and independence. With the specter of

Britain's King George III fresh in their minds, they denounced any system that would concentrate power in a central government. As a compromise to win support from opponents, the framers of the Constitution agreed to add on a bill of rights after ratification to ensure that the rights of states—and their citizens—would be protected.

These assurances helped convince some of the key delegates to vote for the Constitution, and on September 17, 1787, a majority signed the document that would direct a new nation. The delegates called on citizens to meet at state conventions to ratify it. The people in nine of the thirteen states would have to approve the Constitution for it to become law.

While the promise of a bill of rights swayed delegates, ordinary citizens had the final say in the ratification of the Constitution. Many distrusted government; they saw the dangers but not the benefits of a centralized system. To rally popular support for the Constitution, Hamilton, along with James Madison and John Jay, wrote *The Federalist Papers*, a series of letters sent anonymously to newspapers in 1788. Hailed as "the most significant public-relations campaign in history," the letters became key in gaining the public's acceptance of the Constitution and the government it created.

A constitution is ratified

With the vote of the New Hampshire convention—the ninth state to ratify the Constitution—the document became the law of the land on March 4, 1789. (The remaining four states added their approval and by May 1790 all thirteen states had voted in favor of ratifying the new Constitution.) Six months after ratification, on September 25, 1789, Congress fulfilled the promise of a bill of rights and added ten amendments to the original document. These first ten amendments to the Constitution

U.S. CONSTITUTION, TENTH AMENDMENT

The powers not delegated to the United States by the Constitution, nor prohibited by it to the States, are reserved to the States respectively, or to the people.

became the Bill of Rights. Ratified by the states on December 15, 1791, these ten amendments serve as the centerpiece of individual American liberties. The Tenth Amendment in particular sought to ease the fears of those who supported states' rights. It guaranteed that any powers not delegated to the federal government by the Constitution would be "reserved to the States respectively, or to the people." Southern leaders, in particular, wanted to protect states' rights because most feared that a strong national government might try to regulate or ban slavery.

Thomas Jefferson, author of the Declaration of Independence and later president, did not attend the Constitutional Convention. He was serving as U.S. ambassador to France at the time, but he made his views known through letters to Madison and others. Although he supported the Constitution, he did so with reservations, insisting that a bill of rights be included. "A bill of rights," he wrote Madison in 1787, "is what the people are entitled to against every government on earth, general or particular; and what no just government should refuse, or rest on inferences." Congress used many of Jefferson's ideas in the final version of the Bill of Rights.

ENUMERATED V. IMPLIED POWERS

Jefferson and later Andrew Jackson held many of the antifederalists' views regarding individual and states' rights. Jefferson focused his philosophy on the individual rights of humans and believed the nation should rely on agriculture and the work ethic of the farmer. Jefferson's followers adopted the Democratic-Republican label in 1796; the name was shortened to Republican, and later became the Democratic Party under Andrew Jackson's leadership.

Jefferson and the Democratic-Republicans believed that there should be rigid limits on the powers of the federal government. He and his followers called for a strict interpretation of the Constitution that restricted federal powers to those specifically listed, or enumerated, in that document.

Unlike Jefferson, Alexander Hamilton believed that a strict interpretation of the Constitution posed particular difficulties for the new nation. Congress, he believed, needed authority to do its job of governing a nation of powerful and independent states. According to Hamilton, the Constitution granted to Congress both *express* (or enumerated) powers—those specifically listed—and *implied* powers —those that would help Congress accomplish the goals of the express powers. Congress could use implied powers— for example, set up a mint—as long as it was related to efforts approved by the Constitution in an express power— in this case, the power to coin money. Hamilton explained the implied powers doctrine in his writings:

> Thus a corporation may not be erected by Congress for superintending the police of the city of Philadelphia, because they are not authorized to *regulate* the *police* of that city. But one may be erected in relation to

the collection of taxes, or to the trade with foreign counties or to the trade between the States, or with the Indian tribes; because it is the province of the Federal Government to *regulate* those objects, and because it is incident to a general *sovereign* or *legislative* power to *regulate* a thing, to employ all the means which relate to its regulation to the best and greatest advantage.

Shortly after the formation of the new nation, Alexander Hamilton—then Secretary of the Treasury—began a campaign for a federal bank to help ensure sound fiscal policy. The controversy over the bank sparked the first national debate over the Constitution's meaning and how it would be applied. The debate pitted Hamilton's implied powers doctrine against Jefferson's strict interpretation of the Constitution.

Those who favored states' rights objected to the bank because it would give the federal government immense power over the economy. James Madison, who had allied with Hamilton during the campaign to establish a strong national government, parted ways with him over the creation of the bank. Delegates to the Constitutional Convention had rejected Madison's proposal to grant Congress the power to set up corporations. He believed that action had determined the matter, and that Congress could not now legitimately set up a bank corporation. Despite his opposition and that of other leaders, Congress passed legislation in February 1791 to create a federal bank and grant it a twenty-year charter.

Attorney General Edmund Randolph and Secretary of State Thomas Jefferson denounced the measure and tried to persuade President George Washington to veto the bill. They argued that the legislation was unconstitutional

Hamilton, reading the Constitution of the Bank to his f...

ALEXANDER HAMILTON PRESENTS THE CONSTITUTION OF THE FIRST NATIONAL BANK TO MEMBERS OF THE CABINET. AS SECRETARY OF THE TREASURY,

Directors—From Peixotto's painting in the Board Room

HAMILTON LED THE CAMPAIGN TO CREATE A FEDERAL BANK.

congress shall have the power. . .

U.S. Constitution, Article I, Section 8

Section 8. The Congress shall have power to lay and collect taxes, duties, imposts and excises, to pay the debts and provide for the common defence and general welfare of the United States; but all duties, imposts and excises shall be uniform throughout the United States;

To borrow money on the credit of the United States;

To regulate commerce with foreign nations, and among the several states, and with the Indian tribes;

To establish an uniform rule of naturalization, and uniform laws on the subject of bankruptcies throughout the United States;

To coin money, regulate the value thereof, and of foreign coin, and fix the standard of weights and measures;

To provide for the punishment of counterfeiting the securities and current coin of the United States;

To establish post offices and post roads;

To promote the progress of science and useful arts, by securing for limited times to authors and inventors the exclusive right to their respective writings and discoveries;

To constitute tribunals inferior to the Supreme Court;

To define and punish piracies and felonies committed on the high seas, and offences against the law of nations;

To declare war, grant letters of marque and reprisal, and make rules concerning captures on land and water;

To raise and support armies, but no appropriation of money to that use shall be for a longer term than two years;

To provide and maintain a navy;

To make rules for the government and regulation of the land and naval forces;

To provide for calling forth the militia to execute the laws of the union, suppress insurrections and repel invasions;

To provide for organizing, arming, and disciplining, the militia, and for governing such part of them as may be employed in the service of the United States, reserving to the states respectively, the appointment of the officers, and the authority of training the militia according to the discipline prescribed by Congress;

To exercise exclusive legislation in all cases whatsoever, over such District (not exceeding ten miles square) as may, by cession of particular states, and the acceptance of Congress, become the seat of the government of the United States, and to exercise like authority over all places purchased by the consent of the legislature of the state in which the same shall be, for the erection of forts, magazines, arsenals, dock-yards, and other needful buildings;—And

To make all laws which shall be necessary and proper for carrying into execution the foregoing powers, and all other powers vested by this Constitution in the government of the United States, or in any department or officer thereof.

As secretary of state, Thomas Jefferson led the opposition to a national bank. Jefferson would later become the third president of the United States.

because the Constitution had not assigned any such power to Congress. In his argument, Jefferson attacked Hamilton's implied powers doctrine, charging that such a flexible interpretation of the Constitution would give powers to Congress it was never intended to have. "To take a single step beyond the boundaries thus specially drawn around the powers of Congress is to take possession of a boundless field of power, no longer [available to Congress]," Jefferson wrote in "Opinion on the Constitutionality of a National Bank."

Congress was entitled only to those powers specifically listed in the Constitution, he insisted. All other powers were retained by the states and the people, he said. Jefferson based his arguments on the Tenth Amendment, which had won support from a number of states and was headed for ratification along with the rest of the Bill of Rights. The ten amendments would win final ratification later that December.

Jefferson insisted that Congress could not take an action merely because it might "provide for the general welfare of the United States." If that were the case, he noted, "It would reduce the whole instrument [the Constitution] to a single phrase, that of instituting a Congress with power to do whatever would be for the good of the United States; and, as they would be the sole judges of the good or evil, it would be also a power to do whatever evil they please." The very purpose of the Constitution, he argued, was "to lace [Congress] up straitly," so the federal government could not seize total control.

He argued, too, for a strict interpretation of the Constitution's edict that Congress "make all laws *necessary* and proper for carrying into execution the enumerated powers." The bank, he noted might be a "convenient" way for Congress to address financial issues, but it was not "necessary." The nation, he said, could still continue to manage its economy without a federal bank. Jefferson warned that an ingenious debater could find a way to define any action as *convenient*. The framers intentionally used the word *necessary*—in Jefferson's view meaning an action that was required to accomplish a specified objective—to prevent Congress from "swallowing up" all the delegated powers.

In defense of the bank, Hamilton wrote a 15,000-word essay (almost as long as this book) titled "Opinion on the Constitutionality of the Bank of February 23, 1791." In it, he argued that Congress had the power to establish a federal bank under the implied powers doctrine. To govern the nation effectively, he said, Congress must be able "to employ all the means requisite and fairly applicable" to accomplish the goals laid out in the Constitution. That principle, he declared, was "inherent in the very definition of government, and essential to every step of the progress to be made by that of the United States."

Hamilton based his premise on the "necessary and proper" phrase in the Constitution. Those words, he contended, gave Congress implied powers to carry on its work of governing the nation. They empowered the government to take steps to further the nation's goals, as stated in the Constitution.

According to Hamilton, the Constitution never meant to restrict Congress's powers to pass acts that were absolutely essential. Objecting to Jefferson's definition of *necessary*, Hamilton maintained that the word had other, more common, meanings more in keeping with the sense of the Constitution. "Necessary often means no more than needful, requisite, incidental, useful, or conducive to," he said. "The whole turn of the clause containing [the word] indicates, that it was the intent of the Convention, by that clause, to give a liberal latitude to the exercise of the specified powers."

Far from giving government unlimited power as Jefferson claimed, the implied powers doctrine, according to Hamilton, recognized that all government acts had to pass constitutional muster. "For no government has a right to do merely what it pleases," he noted. The test for determining constitutionality, however, did not rest on whether an act was absolutely essential, Hamilton said. "The degree in which a measure is necessary, can never be a test of the legal right to adopt it; that must be a matter of opinion, and can only be a test of expediency." Instead, Hamilton set down his famous test to judge whether an act of Congress was constitutional:

- The action must have a connection to a Congressional power allowed by the Constitution.
- It must be seen as an obvious way of accomplishing the objective of the power.
- It must not be specifically barred by the Constitution.
- It must not infringe on pre-existing rights of states or individuals.

"If the end be clearly comprehended within any of the specified powers, and if the measure have an obvious relation to that end, and is not forbidden by any particular provision of the Constitution, it may safely be deemed to come within the compass of the national authority," Hamilton concluded.

Impressed by Hamilton's forceful argument, Washington signed the bill creating the first Bank of the United States. Hamilton's document set a firm foundation for the implied powers doctrine and a loose interpretation of the Constitution.

THE SECOND UNITED STATES BANK IN PHILADELPHIA AROUND 1830. THE
SUPREME COURT RULING IN *McCulloch* V. *Maryland* ALLOWED THE BANK
TO CONTINUE OPERATIONS DESPITE OPPOSITION FROM THE STATES.

TWO
THE BANK MANAGER'S CASE

THE BANK OF THE UNITED STATES established its headquarters in Philadelphia, the nation's capital at that time, and opened for business on December 12, 1791. Based in part on the venerable Bank of England, the U.S. Bank was financed by $2 million from the federal government and an additional $8 million from private investors. Chief among the investors buying stock in the bank were leading members of Congress.

Eventually eight branches—in Baltimore, Boston, Charleston, New Orleans, New York, Norfolk, Savannah, and Washington, D.C.—served customers nationwide. State banks resented the competition from the federal bank and spread rumors about its operations to stir opposition. In its first year, the bank issued a great number of loans, then recalled many of them. This caused a crash in the stock market, known as the Panic of 1792, as borrowers sold stocks to repay their loans. Alexander Hamilton, as secretary of state, used federal funds to bolster the stock market and stabilize the economy. His efforts succeeded in calming the situation, but the crash intensified criticism of the bank for many years to come.

During its twenty-year operation, the first federal bank accomplished many of its goals. It encouraged business by producing a national paper currency that made it easier and safer for merchants to carry on trade across

As president, James Madison changed his views and supported legislation to create a second federal bank.

state lines and internationally. The bank established a sound credit system that helped people get loans and pay taxes. It also provided loans for the federal government. One of the bank's greatest services to the young nation was its management of the financial transactions involving the Louisiana Purchase. The sale, brokered with France in 1803, doubled the holdings of the United States. Ironically, the land deal facilitated by the bank's existence brought acclaim to Hamilton's old enemy, Thomas Jefferson, who as president pushed through the purchase.

Despite the bank's successes, its detractors continued their demands that it be disbanded. They aimed all kinds of charges against the bank, many of them groundless. By the time the bank's charter came up for renewal in 1811, the Federalists no longer controlled Congress. With popular sentiment against the bank stirred up by its opponents, the ruling Republicans convinced Congress not to renew the bank's charter and it closed on March 3, 1811.

A Second Bank

The War of 1812 the following year brought a renewed call for a central banking system when the War Department could not afford to pay its bills. State and private banks printed money that had little value elsewhere. Counterfeiters flooded the market with worthless bills. Private citizens had difficulty paying bills and cashing in currency for its full value. People hoarded gold and silver, and inflation soared.

The situation became so bad that President James Madison, who had opposed the first bank, agreed to support a second U.S. bank. The track record of the first federal bank had led Madison to revise his views. Its operation for the past twenty years established a precedent, and he no longer believed a national bank was unconstitutional. On April 10, 1816, Congress passed a bill creating the second Bank of the United States. Its charter, granted for twenty years, established an institution much like the first bank. It could issue notes to be redeemed for gold or silver that would be acceptable throughout the nation. Branches of the federal bank, set up in various states, would distribute the national bank notes to help stabilize the financial market and provide citizens with a sound currency. One-fifth of the bank's stock was owned by the federal government; private investors controlled the rest.

In the face of continuing opposition from Republicans, the bank opened for business in several states, loaned money to local banks, and issued federal bank notes. The bank did little to solve the economic woes, including a severe downturn in business that threatened to send the nation into a full-scale depression. Poor management, fraud, and reckless policies led the bank to imminent financial disaster. It called in loans given to state banks, forcing foreclosures on homes and businesses. Outraged citizens joined with longtime opponents of the bank in demanding that it close.

In the wake of these events, eight states passed laws to limit the bank's operations within their borders or to drive it out completely. Indiana and Illinois banned branches of out-of-state banks altogether. The bank's branches in Tennessee, Kentucky, and Ohio were required to pay annual taxes of up to $60,000. In Maryland, the federal bank's branches had to pay a stamp tax on all currency it issued. Alternately, the bank could pay an annual tax of $15,000 to avoid the stamp tax. The law, passed by the state legislature in 1818, applied only to banks chartered outside Maryland. In practice, this meant the federal bank. The Maryland law also offered a reward equal to half the fine for those who reported violators.

James McCulloch, manager of the Baltimore branch of

the federal bank, continued to circulate his bank's notes without paying the state tax or applying the tax stamp on the currency. An informant turned him in. After his arrest, McCulloch was convicted in the County Court of Baltimore County, Maryland, for failing to pay the state tax. The court fined him $2,500, which he refused to pay.

McCulloch then took his case to the Maryland Court of Appeals, which upheld the lower court's decision. The bank manager appealed his conviction to the U.S. Supreme Court. Because the case involved a dispute between federal and state governments and focused on a constitutional question of great importance, the justices agreed to consider it. The Court scheduled oral arguments in the case for February 22, 1819.

Both states' rights advocates and proponents of a strong federal government followed the case closely. They believed, accurately, that the outcome would change the course of the tense battle between states and the federal government for control.

OTHER STATES' RIGHTS CASES

Shortly before hearing arguments in the *McCulloch* case, the Court ruled on two other cases involving states' rights that would make their mark on America's legal legacy and influence the American economy. In both, the Supreme Court overruled state action.

The first case, *Dartmouth College* v. *Woodward*, involved Dartmouth College, a private institution, and the control of a state over private corporations. In 1816 the New Hampshire legislature, under Republican control, decided to convert Dartmouth College, controlled by Federalists, into a state university. To accomplish this, the state changed Dartmouth's charter and the governor appointed new trustees to oversee the school's affairs. The original trustees sued William H. Woodward, secretary of the new

THrOUGH THE court system

First Stop: State Court
Almost all cases (about 95 percent) start in state courts. These courts go by various names, depending on the state in which they operate: circuit, district, municipal, county, or superior. The case is tried and decided by a judge, a panel of judges, or a jury.
The side that loses can then appeal to the next level.

First Stop: Federal Court
U.S. DISTRICT COURT—About 5 percent of cases begin their journey in federal court. Most of these cases concern federal laws, the U.S. Constitution, or disputes that involve two or more states. They are heard in one of the ninety-four U.S. district courts in the nation.
U.S. COURT OF INTERNATIONAL TRADE—Federal court cases involving international trade appear in the U.S. Court of International Trade.
U.S. COURT OF FEDERAL CLAIMS—The U.S. Court of Federal Claims hears federal cases that involve more than $10,000, Indian claims, and some disputes with government contractors.
The loser in federal court can appeal to the next level.

Appeals: State Cases
Forty states have appeals courts that hear cases that have come from the state courts. In states without an appeals court, the case goes directly to the state supreme court.

Appeals: Federal Cases
U.S. CIRCUIT COURT—Cases appealed from U.S. district courts go to U.S. circuit courts of appeals. There are twelve circuit courts that handle cases from throughout the nation. Each district court and every state and territory

are assigned to one of the twelve circuits. Appeals in a few state cases—those that deal with rights guaranteed by the U.S. Constitution—are also heard in this court.

U.S. COURT OF APPEALS—Cases appealed from the U.S. Court of International Trade and the U.S. Court of Federal Claims are heard by the U.S. Court of Appeals for the Federal Circuit. Among the cases heard in this court are those involving patents and minor claims against the federal government.

Further Appeals: State Supreme Court

Cases appealed from state appeals courts go to the highest courts in the state—usually called supreme courts. In New York, the state's highest court is called the court of appeals. Most state cases do not go beyond this point.

Final Appeals: U.S. Supreme Court

The U.S. Supreme Court is the highest court in the country. Its decision on a case is the final word. The Court decides issues that can affect every person in the nation. It has decided cases on slavery, abortion, school segregation, and many other important issues.

The Court selects the cases it will hear—usually around one hundred each year. Four of the nine justices must vote to consider a case in order for it to be heard. Almost all cases have been appealed from the lower courts (either state or federal).

Most people seeking a decision from the Court submit a petition for *certiorari*. Certiorari means that the case will be moved from a lower court to a higher court for review. The Court receives about nine thousand of these requests annually. The petition outlines the case and gives reasons

In rare cases, for example the 1971 case *New York Times* v. *United States*, an issue must be decided immediately. When such a case is of national importance, the Court allows it to bypass the usual lower court system and hears the case directly.

To win a spot on the Court's docket, a case must fall within one of the following categories:

- Disputes between states and the federal government or between two or more states. The Court also reviews cases involving ambassadors, consuls, and foreign ministers.

- Appeals from state courts that have ruled on a federal question.

- Appeals from federal appeals courts (about two-thirds of all requests fall into this category).

board of trustees, to regain control. Daniel Webster and Joseph Hopkinson argued the case on behalf of the college and its original trustees. U.S. Attorney General William Wirt argued on the opposite side, representing the state of New Hampshire in the case. The Court heard oral arguments in March 1818.

In his decision written for the Court, Chief Justice Marshall ruled that states had no authority to interfere with contracts between private parties. A private charter, or contract, did not concern "the political relations between the government and its citizens," as the state contended. Instead, he said, Dartmouth was a private entity and the state had no regulatory authority over it or its charter. The case set limits for the first time on state control over corporate charters. The Supreme Court issued its 6 to 1 decision in *Dartmouth College* v. *Woodward* on February 2, 1819.

The second case, *Sturges* v. *Crowninshield*, also decided in 1819, concerned an 1811 New York law that allowed some debtors to pay only a portion of the amount owed to creditors even if their contracts required full payment. In the early 1800s Richard Crowninshield, a New York businessman, borrowed $1,544 from Josiah Sturges. When Crowninshield's business failed, he filed for bankruptcy under the New York law and started a successful business in Massachusetts. Sturges sued in an effort to force Crowninshield to pay him the money he had borrowed. Sturges claimed that the New York law was unconstitutional and that it interfered with a private contract. After hearing arguments on the case, the Supreme Court overturned the state statute. The law was invalid, according to Chief Justice John Marshall's ruling, because the state had applied it to contracts written before the law went into effect.

The decision also gave federal laws supremacy over

A hand-colored woodcut depicts Eleazar Wheelock, founder of Dartmouth College, teaching in the New Hampshire woods. A landmark Supreme Court case involving the college limited state control over private contracts.

state statutes, a doctrine that would play a prominent role in the *McCulloch* case. Although the Court acknowledged the right of the states to make their own laws on bankruptcy, it ruled that Congress could pass laws that overrode state legislation on the matter. "Where an authority is granted to the Union, to which a similar authority in the States will be absolutely and wholly contradictory and repugnant, then the authority of the Federal Government must be supreme and paramount," Marshall decreed. In other words, Congress had the power, according to the Court, to pass "uniform laws on the subject of bankruptcies," but if state laws conflicted with congressional acts, the federal laws would be "supreme."

The Court delivered its decision on the *Sturges* case on February 17, 1819, two weeks after the *Dartmouth* ruling and three weeks before issuing its decision in *McCulloch v. Maryland*. Observers have called the period "the greatest [five] weeks in the history of the Court."

This woodcut shows British soldiers burning the White House during the War of 1812. Flames also consumed the Capitol, where the U.S. Supreme Court heard cases. After sharing space with Congress in a renovated Capitol, the Supreme Court finally moved into its own building in 1935.

THree
JUSTICES AND ADVOCATES

THE CONSTITUTION CALLED FOR three branches of government: the legislative (Congress), the executive (President), and the judicial (Supreme Court). Congress established the Supreme Court and the system under which it would operate in the Judiciary Act of 1789. When the *McCulloch* case was argued, the U.S. Supreme Court had been in existence for only thirty years.

Originally the Court met in the Royal Exchange building in New York when that city served as the nation's capital in the late 1700s. When the federal government moved its headquarters to Philadelphia in 1791, the Court followed, setting up shop in the Old City Hall. The nation's leaders began the new century in yet another capital city, Washington, D.C. While Congress met in the new Capitol Building, no space had been designated for the Court's use. For several years the Court moved from room to room in the Capitol, sometimes even meeting in homes or taverns when construction forced the justices to find other quarters.

During the War of 1812, the British set fire to the Capitol. On August 24, 1814, British troops stormed into the chambers of the House of Representatives, threw books, furniture, paintings and whatever else they could find into a heap on the floor, sprinkled gun powder into the mix, and set the whole pile on fire. A fierce rainstorm quelled the blaze before the building burned to the ground but not before flames caused major damage to the just-finished Capitol. Reconstruction took several years. In 1819 the justices finally resettled into quarters in the basement of the rebuilt Senate chambers, where a special courtroom had been designed for the Court. The *McCulloch* oral arguments were the first to be heard in the renovated courtroom. The Court stayed in the basement rooms until 1861, when the justices moved upstairs into the old Senate chambers. In 1935 the U.S. Supreme Court moved a final time, into its permanent home in a building of its own across from the Capitol, designed by architect Cass Gilbert.

The Court's basement quarters reflected the judiciary's low position in the newly formed nation. During its first years, the Court had little to do. Justices reviewed cases for only a few weeks each session. In the first decade, the Court decided only sixty cases, about six a year.

Seven members—a chief justice and six associate justices—served on the Supreme Court of the early 1800s. However, only six justices—Gabriel Duvall, William Johnson, Henry Brockholst Livingston, Joseph Story, Bushrod Washington, and Chief Justice John Marshall—heard the *McCulloch* arguments. Justice Thomas Todd, who was ill, did not participate in the case. Five of the seven justices were Democratic-Republicans; Chief Justice Marshall and Justice Washington were the only ones remaining of the Federalists appointed to the Court by Presidents George Washington and John Adams. None of the justices lived full-time in Washington, D.C. They came to the capital for the term aboard ferries, in stage coaches, or on horseback. During particularly stormy weather, justices traveling great distances sometimes did not arrive in Washington in time to hear cases. While serving on the Court, they lived in local boardinghouses, where they ate their meals together while talking over the cases before them.

CHIEF JUSTICE JOHN MARSHALL

Even among the celebrated men who participated in the *McCulloch* case, Chief Justice John Marshall dominated the proceedings. Called the "single most important figure on constitutional law," the Supreme Court's fourth chief justice was appointed to the post by President John Adams in 1801. He served the Court for thirty-four years, during which he wrote 519 opinions and oversaw more than 1,000 cases. From all accounts, his forceful personality—coupled with a superior intellect and high moral character—made him one of the most influential leaders of his time. He drew on his vast knowledge of the law and his exceptional powers of persuasion to sway associate justices to his point of view.

The oldest of fifteen children, Marshall was born in 1755 and grew up in the Blue Ridge foothills of Virginia. His father, a friend of George Washington, worked as a surveyor. His mother was a distant relative of Thomas Jefferson. The family, like those of other farmers in the region, owned slaves. He fought in the Revolutionary War, served in the Virginia House of Delegates, and practiced law in Richmond. After a short stint as Virginia's representative in Congress, he accepted President Adams's offer to serve as secretary of state. Shortly afterward, the president appointed him as chief justice. He held the position longer than any other chief justice in American history. He was sixty-three when the Court heard the *McCulloch* arguments.

Marshall was an unpretentious, affectionate man with an engaging personality that attracted people to him. He liked to walk and read, play chess and compete in an early game of horseshoes known as quoits, but he particularly enjoyed sociable gatherings with friends, who were drawn

LIFE AS A SUPREME COURT JUSTICE IN THE 1800S

U.S. Supreme Court justices had a rigorous schedule in the first half of the 1800s when the *McCulloch* case was tried. In addition to the duties required by the Supreme Court, each justice was assigned to at least one circuit court. This meant that the justice not only had to travel to Washington, D.C., to attend Supreme Court hearings and conferences during the winter months; he also had to travel from town to town presiding at circuit courts under his jurisdiction. Justices also sat with district court judges to hear appeals. Associate Justice Joseph Story, for example, traveled more than two thousand miles a year to dispense justice in the circuit courts of Maine, New Hampshire, Rhode Island, and Massachusetts. Before automobiles, interstate commuter trains, and air travel, justices rode on horseback or in horse-drawn carriages over often-dangerous roads.

The Supreme Court originally had six members, but a seventh justice was added in 1807 to help with the workload. In 1837 the Court expanded to nine members, and from 1863 to 1865 ten justices served on the Court. Opponents of President Jackson reduced the seats on the Court to nine, then eight in 1866 and 1867. Finally, in 1869 Congress set the number of Supreme Court justices at nine, the size it remains today.

During the early 1800s, most of the justices stayed in boardinghouses along Pennsylvania Avenue when the Supreme Court was in session. Among the more noted was Elizabeth Peyton's house at the intersection of Pennsylvania Avenue and 4 1/2 Street (now called Fourth Street S.W.). There Chief Justice John Marshall, Justice Story

Senators John C. Calhoun, and Henry Clay, among others, spent their evenings discussing the issues of the day.

Chief Justice Marshall encouraged his fellow justices to live together at the same boardinghouse during Court sessions. Marshall believed that such living arrangements brought justices closer together and led to unanimous decisions. Such appeared to be the case; the Marshall Court handed down one unanimous ruling after another during the course of almost thirty-five years.

According to Justice Story, he and his colleagues spent many evenings discussing cases at the boardinghouse:

[We] live in the most frank and unaffected inti-
macy . . . united as one, with a mutual esteem
which makes even the labors of jurisprudence
light . . . we [discuss] every question as we pro-
ceed, and familiar conferences at our lodgings
often come to a very quick and, I trust, a very accurate opinion, in a few hours.

All was not work, however. Story noted, "Our social hours . . . are passed in gay and frank conversation."

to his charm and sweet nature. Tall and thin, he paid little attention to his attire and often wore rumpled clothes that did not match—perhaps a remnant of his rustic upbringing. If his clothes were sometimes shabby, his intellect was not. His analytic mind enabled him to translate complex principles and theories into clear language that everyone could understand.

The decisions of the Marshall Court gave form to the new government, empowered Congress, and intervened in the power struggle between states and the federal government. An ardent Federalist who had lobbied for passage of the Constitution, Marshall molded the Court into an equal partner with the other branches of government. Under his guidance, the Supreme Court used its power to overturn laws that—in the judgment of the Court—violated the Constitution.

This power of judicial review, established in the 1803 case of *Marbury* v. *Madison*, became established doctrine. The case involved the attempt by John Adams to pack the courts with Federalists in the last hours of his presidency. Many of the appointments, however, did not get issued before Democratic-Republican Thomas Jefferson assumed power. William Marbury, one of the Federalist appointees, sued Secretary of State James Madison to issue his commission as a justice of the peace. Marbury relied on a section of the Judiciary Act of 1789 which gave the Supreme Court power to issue a judicial order requiring public officials to perform their duties. The Court under Marshall's leadership overturned the pertinent section in the Judiciary Act, ruling that it gave the Court powers not granted in the Constitution. While this cut back the Court's power, the rest of the decision authorized the Court to decide which laws were unconstitutional. The ruling put the Court on equal footing with the other two branches of government.

Marshall also dramatically changed the way the Supreme Court operated. He discouraged justices from issuing separate opinions on cases as had been the practice in the past. Instead, the Court began issuing one majority opinion, which Marshall usually wrote. The justices expressed differing views during informal discussions at the boardinghouse where they all stayed while Court was in session. In the face of Marshall's policy, however, associate justices rarely voiced opposition or stated their views in public.

JUSTICE WILLIAM JOHNSON

Justice William Johnson was one of the few who issued dissents. Known as the Supreme Court's "first great dissenter," Justice Johnson often opposed the views of Marshall and his fellow associates. Appointed to the Court by Jefferson in 1804, he became the first Democratic-Republican justice. Before his nomination, the Charleston lawyer served several years as a South Carolina legislator and a judge on the state's highest court.

Serious and thin-skinned, Johnson often riled the other members of the Court—particularly Justice Story—with his combativeness and lack of tact. John Quincy Adams called him a "restless, turbulent, hot-headed, politician," but also "a man of considerable talents." Johnson's talent for clear reasoning contributed to the Court's work. During thirty years as a Supreme Court justice, he wrote almost half the dissents and two-thirds of the concurrences issued by the Court. Johnson supported states' rights but also opposed state limits on commerce. He later became a strong defender of the Union in the face of threats by the Southern states to secede. Among the youngest justices, he was forty-seven at the time the bank case was heard.

JUSTICE GABRIEL DUVALL

A quiet man with a courtly manner, Justice Gabriel Duvall, at sixty-six, was the oldest justice on the Court. The associate justice had begun to lose his hearing by the time of the *McCulloch* case and had difficulty following oral arguments. The other justices regarded the older man with affection, according to one historian. Justice Duvall lived fairly close to the Court, traveling from his estate in Maryland, about fifty miles from the capital. He did not often express strong views on issues and wrote only seventeen opinions during nearly twenty-four years on the Court. Perhaps Duvall's most valuable contribution was his skill as a diplomat. He often calmed resentments by restating another justice's harsh statements in more tactful terms. Although he was a Democratic-Republican nominated to the post by President James Madison, Duvall almost always voted with Chief Justice Marshall in support of a strong national government. Duvall had served as the first comptroller of the currency under President Thomas Jefferson. He was chief judge of the Maryland General Court for six years before his nomination to the Supreme Court.

JUSTICE HENRY BROCKHOLST LIVINGSTON

Justice Henry Brockholst Livingston, like Duvall, was considered one of the Court's "silent" members. During his sixteen years on the Court, he never wrote a majority opinion. Yet, also like Duvall, he helped ease tensions among justices that threatened to divide the Court. Noted for his quick wit, Livingston was far from silent during the spirited debates over the boardinghouse table. He eagerly shared his views on a variety of issues, offered scholarly observations on cases, and entertained his fellow justices with his good humor. Livingston came from a well-connected New York family and served as a state assembly member and as a justice on that state's highest court. He had been involved in a duel in 1798, killing his opponent. Another Jefferson nominee, Livingston had taken a strong antifederalist stance earlier in his career, but he supported the cause of a national government as a Supreme Court justice. He was sixty-one when the Court considered the *McCulloch* case.

JUSTICE BUSHROD WASHINGTON

Justice Bushrod Washington, along with Chief Justice Marshall, represented the Federalist Party on the Court. At fifty-six, he was among the older justices on the Court during the *McCulloch* proceedings. A nephew of George Washington, he took office in 1799 after being appointed to the post by John Adams. Considered by most historians to be an undistinguished member of the Court, Washington has been described as a "short, untidy man who liked snuff and suffered from ill health."

A lawyer and teacher who had attended the College of William and Mary with Chief Justice Marshall, Washington became a close ally of the chief justice. He voted against Marshall in only three cases during the more than thirty years they served on the Court together. His fellow jurists respected his views and gave weight to his comments during discussions about cases. A firm believer that the Court should present a unified front whenever possible, he seemed content to present his views—based on logic and precedent—at the justices' informal gatherings, and let Marshall write the opinions. Although himself authored few Supreme Court opinions, Washington wrote detailed reports of the cases he heard in his other job as circuit court judge. At that time, all the associate justices were required to ride a circuit and hear cases within their territory in addition their duties on the Supreme Court.

Washington stayed with the other justices at the

boardinghouse while the Court was in session, although he lived only sixteen miles away at Mount Vernon, the estate he inherited from his uncle after his aunt's death. He freed the estate's slaves according to his uncle's wishes, but caused a stir when he brought his own slaves to the plantation and later sold them to pay off debts. As a member of the American Colonization Society, however, the justice supported efforts to set up a colony in Africa as a home for free black Americans.

JUSTICE JOSEPH STORY

The youngest person ever to serve as a Supreme Court justice, Joseph Story was only thirty-nine when the bank case came before the Court. At age thirty-two Story was appointed to the Court by President James Madison in 1811 on the same day as Justice Duvall. A Massachusetts native, he was a Democratic-Republican but became a close friend and ally of Chief Justice Marshall during his years on the Court. Brilliant, learned, and energetic, Story had a tendency to deliver long monologues on the issues he cared about. He and Justice Johnson clashed frequently, arguing heatedly over cases during the informal discussions at the boardinghouse. He supported Marshall's efforts to strengthen the federal judiciary and wrote some of the major decisions furthering that goal. His landmark decisions on commerce helped shaped the nation's economic growth and promoted trade between states.

Story graduated from Harvard second in his class and served in the Massachusetts legislature for several years and briefly in the U.S. Congress before his nomination to the Supreme Court. Later he became the guiding force behind the creation of Harvard Law School. He also advocated the education of women. Story despised slavery, a view he made clear in his 1822 circuit court decision involving *La Jeune Eugenie*, a vessel thought to have been

JUSTICE JOSEPH STORY WAS THE YOUNGEST PERSON EVER TO SERVE ON THE
U.S. SUPREME COURT.

involved in the slave trade. Even so, the Massachusetts native believed that the Constitution allowed slavery and that it could be abolished gradually only through changing the nation's laws. Justice Story's commentaries and extensive correspondence provide an intriguing look into the workings of the early Court. His scholarly writings on the Constitution and U.S. law greatly influenced legal thinking of the nineteenth century and made him "the foremost of American legal writers."

JUSTICE THOMAS TODD

Ill health and bad travel conditions often prevented Justice Thomas Todd from attending oral arguments. During his time on the Court, he wrote only fourteen opinions and missed five sessions, including the 1819 term during which *McCulloch* was decided. Todd, who was fifty-four in 1819, had made a fortune in land speculation in the West and had been among the leaders in the campaign for Kentucky's statehood. He served on the first Kentucky Supreme Court before being named to the U.S. Supreme Court. A Democratic-Republican like most of the other members of the Court, Todd was appointed by President Jefferson in 1807.

LEGAL GIANTS

The six advocates arguing the *McCulloch* case before the Supreme Court were among the nation's most brilliant lawyers. Speaking on behalf of the federal government and the bank were three of the most renowned legal stars ever to argue before the Court: Daniel Webster, U.S. Attorney General William Wirt, and William Pinkney. Maryland, defending states' rights, enlisted three other notables: Joseph Hopkinson, Maryland Attorney General Luther Martin, and Walter Jones. These six men, according to Brigham Young University President Rex E.

Lee, represented "perhaps the greatest collection of prominent advocates in the history of [the Supreme] Court's bar."

Daniel Webster

Daniel Webster's reputation as an orator attracted packed audiences to courtrooms where he presented cases. A Federalist and strong supporter of a national government, Webster performed in the courtroom as an actor before an adoring audience. One of the most notable celebrities of his day, he dressed for court in a fashionable blue coat with oversized brass buttons.

Webster was born in New Hampshire in 1782. After graduating from Dartmouth, he opened a law office in his home state in 1807. He soon became known as a leader in the Federalist Party and won election to Congress in 1812, where he served as New Hampshire's representative until 1816. In 1823, he returned to Congress as a Massachusetts senator after moving to that state.

During the intervening years, Webster won fame as the eloquent advocate for a strong national government in many of the major cases to reach the Supreme Court on the issue. He and Chief Justice Marshall became the main champions of the cause and, on several occasions, Marshall used Webster's phrases in his decisions. Only thirty-seven when he defended the Bank of the United States, the lawyer argued 185 cases in the Supreme Court, second only to Walter Jones. Webster's performance in the cases established him as the nation's foremost constitutional lawyer. The lawyer's grand style of speaking, combining eloquence with evidence, inspired audiences everywhere. His fame as an orator was so well known that Steven Vincent Benét used Webster as a character in his 1938 play, *The Devil and Daniel Webster*, in which the legendary lawyer defended a farmer who sold his soul to the devil. President

John F. Kennedy, in his book *Profiles in Courage*, noted Webster's "ability to make alive and supreme the latent sense of oneness, of Union, that all Americans felt but which few could express."

Webster later ran unsuccessfully for president as one of three Whig candidates against Democrat Martin Van Buren, served twice as U.S. Secretary of State, and took a leading role in efforts to preserve the Union in the explosive years leading up to the Civil War.

U.S. ATTORNEY GENERAL WILLIAM WIRT

Until 1870 when Congress created the post of solicitor general to act as lead counsel for the United States, the attorney general filled that role. As the nation's ninth attorney general, a post he held for twelve years, William Wirt participated in more landmark Supreme Court rulings than any other advocate, at least in the nineteenth century. Those cases—including *Dartmouth College* v. *Woodward*, *McCulloch* v. *Maryland*, *Cohens* v. *Virginia*, and many more—numbered among the most important in the nation's history, defining as they did the American system of government.

Born in Maryland in 1772, Wirt was admitted to the bar in 1792. His first big case came when President Thomas Jefferson appointed him to prosecute Aaron Burr for treason. He lost that case to Luther Martin, but his four-hour speech during the trial brought him fame for his eloquence, polished wit, and clear logic. He served as U.S. attorney general under two presidents, James Monroe, who first appointed him to the post in 1817, and John Quincy Adams. A handsome man with clear blue eyes and sandy curls, Wirt often appeared in court wearing a swallowtail coat and fashionable vest, tie, and breeches. He was forty-six when he presented the federal government's arguments in the *McCulloch* case.

Though he lacked the brilliance of Pinkney and the magnetism of Webster, Wirt succeeded through persistence and hard work. Using logic and analytical reasoning, he carefully laid a foundation for his arguments. His voice was his most effective tool. Musical and "hauntingly melodious," it captured the attention of his audience, according to historian John B. Boles. "With an artist's feel for sound and metaphor Wirt constructed verbal symphonies. Mixing poetry with law, literature with history, with a dash of wit and a ready smile, Wirt appeals to the intellect and emotions of his hearers," Boles wrote. Jurors related to Wirt, who was once described as "the most beloved of American advocates." Salmon Chase, chief justice of the U.S. Supreme Court from 1864 to 1873, said the lawyer was "one of the purest and noblest of men." In his eulogy for Wirt in 1834, John Quincy Adams called him a man with "a brilliant imagination, a discerning intellect, a sound judgment and indefatigable capacity, and vigorous energy of application."

WILLIAM PINKNEY

Perhaps the most celebrated lawyer of his time, William Pinkney presented a paradox of superlatives and negatives. Henry Wheaton, Court reporter and the author of a generally flattering biography of Pinkney, described the flamboyant lawyer and former U.S. attorney general as being "one of the brightest and meanest of mankind." Pinkney was indisputably brilliant; he spent hundreds of hours preparing for a case, rehearsing each word until every syllable of his recitation had the correct intonation. His grasp of the subject was phenomenal and his eloquence legendary. A devoted corps of fans often came to court just to hear him speak and left as soon as he finished his oration.

According to accounts of the day, Pinkney himself was his own biggest fan. Notorious for his vanity and arrogance, the lawyer sought applause almost as much as a victory in court. He directed his performances to the audience, wore a corset in an effort to appear trim and youthful, and dressed in the latest fashion, including "amber-colored doeskin gloves," which he kept on while addressing the Court. He was fifty-four at the time of the Court hearing on the *McCulloch* case.

But even detractors who envied his success had to acknowledge his eminence and consummate skill as an attorney. Chief Justice John Marshall said that Pinkney was "the greatest man he had ever seen in a Court of Justice." Marshall's successor, Chief Justice Roger B. Taney, gave a similar review of the lawyer's abilities: "I have heard almost all the great advocates of the United States, both of the past and present generation, but I have seen none equal to him." Similarly, Justice Story wrote of the lawyer, "Every time I hear him he rises higher and higher in my estimation. His clear and forcible manner of putting his case before the Court, his powerful and commanding eloquence, occasionally illumined with sparkling lights but always logical and appropriate, and above all, his accurate and discriminating Law knowledge, which he pours out with wonderful precision, give him in my opinion, a great superiority over every man whom I have known."

MARYLAND ATTORNEY GENERAL LUTHER MARTIN

Facing this stellar cast, the lawyers representing Maryland in the *McCulloch* case had impressive credentials of their own. A leader of the American bar during the nation's infancy, Maryland Attorney General Luther Martin had long championed states' rights. As a delegate from Maryland to the Constitutional Convention, he refused to sign the Constitution because he believed it violated states' rights. After walking out of the convention in protest, Martin worked to defeat ratification of the Constitution. He later allied with the Federalists because of his hatred for Thomas Jefferson, an antifederalist. Jefferson once called Martin "the federal bulldog."

Not known as an orator, Martin nevertheless made his mark as a formidable advocate. He served as Maryland's attorney general for twenty-seven years before resigning to resume private practice. During that time, he successfully served as defense lawyer in two of the nation's most famous trials: the 1805 impeachment of his friend, Supreme Court Justice Samuel Chase, and the 1807 treason trial of Aaron Burr. In a tour de force that capped his career, Martin won Chase's acquittal before a tribunal in which a majority belonged to the opposition party. The verdict was a major defeat for President Thomas Jefferson, one of the leaders in the effort to oust Chase. U.S. Attorney General William Wirt, who would later argue against Martin in the *McCulloch* case, served as chief prosecutor at Burr's trial. Angered at the outcome of that case, Baltimore residents hanged Martin—and Chief Justice John Marshall—in effigy. The protesters labeled Martin "Lawyer Brandy-Bottle," no doubt a reference to the attorney's fondness for drink. At least one judge threatened to jail him for his drunken behavior. Martin's extensive knowledge of the law and his aggressive defense strategies, however, earned him respect as an attorney and success in court. He operated the largest law practice in Maryland.

In 1818, Martin returned to serve for three more years as Maryland's state attorney general. He was seventy-one when he argued Maryland's cause in the *McCulloch* case. Ironically, the *McCulloch* case put Martin on the side of his hated adversary, Jefferson.

JOSEPH HOPKINSON

Like other participants in the *McCulloch* case, Joseph Hopkinson, attorney for Maryland, was a leading figure of the time. A prominent Philadelphia lawyer, Hopkinson had graduated from the University of Pennsylvania in 1786 and was admitted to the bar in 1791. His father, Francis Hopkinson, had signed the Declaration of Independence; his wife was the daughter of the governor of Pennsylvania. A Federalist, Hopkinson served two terms in the U.S. House, representing the state of Pennsylvania, where he was born.

Hopkinson had worked with Martin before, in the successful defense of Supreme Court Justice Samuel Chase in the jurist's 1805 impeachment trial. He had also partnered with Webster, as an associate representing Dartmouth College in its landmark Supreme Court case the year before. The decision in that case, favoring Dartmouth, had been announced just three weeks earlier. Hopkinson's services were in demand: in 1819, the year he represented Maryland in *McCulloch*, he also worked on a third Supreme Court case, *Sturges* v. *Crowninshield*. Hopkinson, forty-eight at the time of the bank hearing, later became a federal judge for the Eastern District of Pennsylvania. For all his success as a lawyer, Hopkinson is perhaps best known for writing the words to the song "Hail Columbia," the nation's first anthem.

WALTER JONES

At the time of the *McCulloch* case Walter Jones was forty-three years old and serving as U.S. attorney for the District of Columbia, a post he held for nineteen years. Jones would become an old warrior in legal circles, eventually arguing 317 cases before the U.S. Supreme Court during his long career—more than any other lawyer. His performance before the Court was said to be "durable though unspectacular."

The perennial advocate was a small man, "well built and active," according to his grandson. He was not particularly handsome, but expressive brown eyes lit up his face and his voice was "rich and clear." He spoke with such distinctness that his words could easily be heard even before a large gathering.

DANIEL WEBSTER DEFENDS THE UNION DURING A SPEECH IN THE SENATE REBUTTING SENATOR ROBERT HAYNE'S CONTENTION THAT STATES' RIGHTS SHOULD REIGN SUPREME. IN THE *McCULLOCH* CASE, WEBSTER TOOK A SIMILAR STANCE, DEFENDING THE FEDERAL GOVERNMENT'S POWER TO ESTABLISH A NATIONAL BANK OVER THE OBJECTIONS OF INDIVIDUAL STATES.

four
BEFORE THE COURT

THE oral arguments extended over a week and a half, beginning with Daniel Webster's exhortations on February 22, 1819, and ending with William Pinkney's conclusion on March 3. Because of the magnitude of the issues raised by the case, the Court allowed more than one advocate per side to present oral arguments.

For nine days, the six advocates stood before the black-garbed justices and pled their cases. Pinkney used a third of that time—a full three days—to state his views. At that time, justices did not pose questions during oral arguments. Lawyers delivered well-rehearsed speeches before the Court and the audience gathered for the performance. And what a performance it was! Pinkney and Webster both were well-known for playing to the gallery. Lawyers dressed for the part, gestured dramatically to emphasize points, and modulated their voices to draw attention to their words. At times the courtroom resembled a theater as advocates gave eloquent orations, and audience members responded with approving or disapproving murmurs.

The courtroom was the place to be for anyone with social aspirations. According to legal historian Charles Warren, "the social season of Washington began with the opening of the Supreme Court Term." The case had captured the attention of businessmen and leaders in the financial world as well as politicians and socialites. Justice Story recorded in his notes of the proceeding that the courtroom was packed "almost to suffocation." He described a "crowded audience of ladies and gentlemen," so crammed that many could not find seats and were turned away.

The importance of the case and the stellar reputation of the advocates gained the attention of the press as well. The February 25, 1819, edition of the Washington, D.C., *National Intelligencer* reported the ongoing arguments to an interested public:

> The argument has involved some of the most important principles of constitutional law which have been discussed with an equal degree of learning and eloquence and have constantly attracted the attention of a numerous and intelligent auditor by whom the final [decision] of this most important question from the Supreme Tribunal is anxiously expected.

No sound could be heard in the packed courtroom as Daniel Webster rose to make the government's case. Long noted as a formidable orator, the lawyer from Massachusetts used his considerable debating skills to persuade the justices of his position. He would focus on two questions:

> • Whether the Constitution allowed Congress to incorporate a federal bank; and
> • Whether the states had the power to tax it.

Since there were no tape recordings in that day and no verbatim record exists of the oral arguments, we rely on

Briefs and Not-So-Brief Arguments

The U.S. Supreme Court did not require lawyers to submit briefs, or written arguments, on their cases until 1821. Lawyers were expected to provide the justices only with a statement outlining the points of the case. The real work of the Court relied on the oral arguments, during which lawyers explained the details of the case and advocated their views. For that reason, Court hearings on individual cases sometimes continued for days, as lawyers expounded on the issues and explored every argument possible.

In 1821 the Court began requiring lawyers to file briefs. Apparently not all lawyers followed the requirement, because in 1849 the Court ruled that lawyers who did not file briefs would not be allowed to participate in oral arguments. Until that time, the Court continued its reliance on oral arguments as the primary source of information on a case. But beginning in 1849, the Court limited each side to two hours of arguments. Today, with one hundred or so cases to be heard every year, the Court allots lawyers on each side only one-half hour to make their point.

Few of the early briefs exist, though rare copies of notes kept by lawyers have shed light on some cases. Not until 1870, eighty years after the first Court convened, did the judicial branch preserve the complete record of the motions, briefs, and documents of cases before the Supreme Court.

Oral arguments have proved to be even more transitory. For many of the early cases, only the Court reporter's summary of the oral arguments has survived. Occasionally observers took notes of the proceedings; in addition to commentary on the cases, the reports preserved a few of the actual words spoken by the advocates in the Supreme Court's first cases. Most of those stirring words—as well as the more mundane passages—are gone forever.

With the advent of tape recordings, the oral arguments of those pleading their case before the nation's high court have been preserved. Since 1955, audiotapes or transcripts or both provide an accurate rendering of the arguments made before the Court. Historians can now hear beyond the words, to the lawyers' inflections, as they try to convince the justices of the rightfulness of their cause. They can also listen to the sometimes ironic or argumentative tones of the justices' questions, the humorous banter, and even asides that would not have been otherwise preserved.

the summary of the proceedings produced by Henry Wheaton, the Court's reporter.

Taxation: A Power to Destroy

Webster began by arguing that the issue of a federal bank had already been settled nearly thirty years ago when Congress first established a U.S. bank. Before approving the

Act of February 5, 1791, which incorporated a federal bank, the first Congress debated the issue thoroughly, according to Webster. "The arguments . . . in favour of this power, were stated, and exhausted, in that discussion," Webster told the Court. In addition, he said, each Congress since had operated on the assumption that the federal bank was legal.

"Individuals, it is true, have doubted, or thought otherwise," Webster conceded. But, he noted, all three branches of government had accepted the power of Congress to create a national bank. "The executive government has acted upon it; and the courts of law have acted upon it," Webster said. Even many of those who opposed the act of 1791 had since accepted the outcome, according to the government's lawyer.

"When all branches of the government have thus been acting on the existence of this power [to incorporate a federal bank] nearly thirty years, it would seem almost too late to call it in question," Webster stated. The only reason to revisit the question, he noted, would be if it were "plain and manifest" that such power violated the Constitution. And it did not, according to Webster. The Constitution vested Congress with "certain powers," he argued, including the power to raise money and to declare wars. In order to carry out those tasks, Webster contended, the Constitution allowed Congress to do whatever was needed, as long as the actions were not specifically banned. In other words, Congress could adopt new technologies to wage wars—or to raise revenue, even though the founders had not listed them in the Constitution. "Steam frigates, for example, were not in the minds of those who framed the constitution, as among the means to naval warfare," Webster noted. "But no one doubts the power of Congress to use them, as means to an authorized end." Likewise, he noted, Congress had the power to establish a bank to carry out its legitimate task of running the government—even if the founders had not contemplated a federal bank.

Quoting the Constitution, Webster stated that Congress had the power "to make all laws which shall be necessary and proper" to carrying out its duties as authorized by the Constitution. That section, he argued, gave Congress the power to take suitable steps to fulfill its tasks. And Congress had the power to determine which steps to take, he said. If Congress's actions were limited only to those considered "absolutely indispensable" to the task at hand, then little would get done. "The government would hardly exist," Webster claimed; "at least, it would be wholly inadequate to the purposes of its formation."

A federal bank, Webster contended, was "a proper and suitable instrument to assist the operations of the government, in the collection and disbursement of the revenue; in the occasional anticipations of taxes and [fees]; and in the regulation of the actual currency, as being a part of the trade and exchange between the States." It was Congress's role—not the Court's—to decide whether the creation of a federal bank was the best way to manage such operations, Webster argued. The only question the Court should legitimately consider, the lawyer said, was whether a federal bank *could* help Congress fulfill its duties.

Secondly, Webster disputed the power of the states to tax the federal bank. The Constitution, he noted, established that "the Constitution itself, and the laws passed in pursuance of its provisions" were "the supreme law of the land." As such, they superseded state laws and state constitutions; even if a state law required actions opposite those stipulated by a federal statute, the federal law overrode the state provisions. If a dispute arose between states and the federal government, the Constitution gave the U.S. Supreme Court the power to decide the matter.

In the *McCulloch* case, Webster said, the Court had to

decide whether the state's tax on the bank interfered with its operation. "This question seems answered as soon as it is stated," Webster told the justices. If states had the power to tax federal property, he argued, they could control the U.S. government. "An unlimited power to tax involves, necessarily, a power to destroy," Webster said, "because there is a limit beyond which no institution and no property can bear taxation."

He pointed out that even in the much-weaker system of the confederation, states could not tax property owned by the federal government. "Is it supposed that property of the United States is now subject to the power of the State governments, in a greater degree than under the Confederation?" Webster asked the Court. He foresaw all kinds of problems if the states were allowed to tax the federal government. States unhappy with rulings from federal courts could use taxes to force the courts to close down and leave. Maryland could impose taxes on other federal activities, closing down the custom house—and interstate travel and commerce.

Webster argued that Maryland had not taxed the bank based on profits or income. Rather, the state had imposed fees to limit circulation of the bank's currency. "It narrows and abridges the powers of the bank in a manner which, it would seem, even Congress could not do," he said. Maryland based its law on "principles and reasoning which would subject every important measure of the national government to the revision and control of the State legislatures."

Congress authorized the bank to issue bills above five dollars. Such bills, according to U.S. law, were to be honored in payment of all debts due the government. Webster noted that Maryland's law made it a crime for anyone to use the bank's currency unless it had been stamped by the state (for a fee). The state law raised money for the state by

adding to the cost of the federal bank's bills. Whether
Maryland intended to raise money or to expel the bank
from the state, the law interfered with federal revenue,
Webster said. "There cannot be a clearer case of interfer-
ence," he told the Court. "The bank cannot exist, nor can
any bank established by Congress exist, if this right to tax
it exists in the State governments." For the federal government to surrender such power to state governments would
be to give up "those fundamental and essential powers
without which the government cannot be maintained,"
Webster said.

The case was not just about a federal bank, the lawyer
noted. The U.S. government could survive without a bank,
he conceded. But, he argued, the federal government
could not exist unless Congress could "exercise its constitutional powers, at its own discretion, without being
subject to the control of State legislation." State governments, he noted, should not be able to second-guess constitutional acts of Congress, nor should states be allowed
impede federal legislation. It was late in the day when
Webster ended his arguments and at last sat down. Elec-
tric lights had not yet been invented, so kerosene lamps
provided a soft glow in the darkening hours of the after-
noon. No red light blinked to warn the speaker that his
time had ended. Each attorney spoke until he had made
his case.

MARYLAND MAKES ITS CASE

Joseph Hopkinson took his place before the Court to
present Maryland's position. The lawyer addressed three
questions:

> • Did Congress have the power, under the Constitu-
> tion, to incorporate the federal bank?
> • Did the bank, on its own authority, have the right to

JOSEPH HOPKINSON ARGUED THE CASE FOR MARYLAND. ALTHOUGH A SKILLED
LAWYER, HOPKINSON WAS BEST KNOWN FOR WRITING THE LYRICS TO THE SONG
"HAIL COLUMBIA."

set up branches in the states?
- Could the bank claim exemption from state taxes?

Like Webster, Hopkinson began by exploring the constitutional question. Unlike the attorney for the United States, however, Maryland's advocate argued that approval of the first federal bank did not mean that the second bank should also be approved. Conceding that the first bank established by Congress may well have been "necessary and proper" to raise money for the fledgling nation, Hopkinson argued that the U.S. government no longer needed a bank. In 1819, he noted, "many facilities for money transactions abound" that were not available in the early days of the republic. The first federal bank, Hopkinson said, met three essential needs as defined by Alexander Hamilton:

- added to the nation's capital by creating paper currency based on gold and silver;
- gave the government quick access to funds, especially important during an emergency; and
- made it easier for citizens to pay their taxes by loaning them money and speeding up bank transactions from place to place.

Because the first bank served a necessary purpose in meeting those needs, its creation fell under the Constitution's requirements. If the second bank could not meet the same test, Hopkinson said, then it would not be allowed under the Constitution. According to the lawyer, the second bank failed the test. Congress could no longer justify a federal bank as necessary because public banks located in every state served the same purposes. In 1791, when Congress authorized the first bank, only three banks existed in the United States, Hopkinson said. The three banks had little capital and limited operations. "Very different is the case now," he told the justices. In 1819, he continued, public banks had spread over the country, providing adequate and convenient service to their customers. The state banks had a good track record as well, meeting the nation's needs for five years after the first federal bank's charter expired and before Congress established the second bank.

"Whatever might have been the truth and force of the bank argument in 1791," Hopkinson said, "they were wholly wanting in 1816 [when Congress created the second bank]."

He proceeded to his second argument. Even if Congress met all the constitutional requirements in creating the federal bank, that did not give the bank automatic authority to set up branches in the states, Hopkinson contended. According to the lawyer, the bank had to prove that opening branches was constitutionally necessary—that the state offices *had* to be set up in order to serve the nation's needs. Such proof, Hopkinson argued, did not exist. "Branches are not necessary for any of the enumerated advantages," he told the Court. The federal bank could create paper currency and provide quick access to money without branches. State banks could, and did, circulate the government's currency, providing loans and speeding bank transactions.

Hopkinson charged that the bank directors and its stockholders, not the government, benefited from the branches. Should the state's right to regulate and tax a money-making business be overruled, Hopkinson asked, in favor of a group of men "who have no concern, and no duty, but to increase their profits?"

And who, the lawyer asked, should determine whether the branches served a constitutionally necessary function? The question should be settled by Congress, whose members represent the interests of the states, not by appointed bank officials. Otherwise, he said, "we have really spent a great deal of labour and learning to very little purpose, in our attempt to establish a form of government in which the powers of those who govern shall be strictly defined and controlled."

Hopkinson contended that allowing the bank to set up branches in a state—without the state's assent and "without regard to its interests, its policy, or institutions"—flouted the state's rights even more than the creation of the bank did. A central bank, he noted, would "interfere less with the rights and policy of the States, than those wide spreading branches, planted every where, and influencing all the business of the community." If the government allowed institutions to disregard states' rights, Hopkinson said, at least Congress should justify the need for such measures. The decision, he argued, should not be left in the hands of bank directors.

A STATE'S RIGHT TO TAX

If states had to go along with such a scheme, they should at least have the power to tax the bank's branches as they would any other entity, Hopkinson reasoned in presenting his third argument. According to the Constitution, states held any rights not specifically reserved for the federal government, Hopkinson noted. "The right now assailed by the bank, is the right of taxing property within the property of the State. This is the highest attribute of sovereignty, the right to raise revenue; in fact, the right to exist; without which no other right can be held or enjoyed. The general power to tax is not denied to the States, but the bank claims to be exempted from the operation of this power," he said.

Both the state and federal governments had traditionally taxed bank property. Nothing about the federal bank's assets set it apart from other corporations that had to pay Maryland taxes, according to the lawyer. Furthermore, he argued, the United States government did not control the bank; bank directors ran the corporation. It acted as any other bank; only its name as a federal bank set it apart from other banks. That did not justify its exemption from state taxes, Hopkinson said.

He noted that the federal government had to obtain a state's consent to locate other federal operations on its soil. And in those cases—forts, arsenals, and other defense outposts—the federal government maintained control over the facilities. The bank, Hopkinson said, did not ask permission to set up business in Maryland, setting itself above state authority, territorial rights, and "demands of the public revenue."

The Constitution, in the tenth section of the first article, limited the state's right to levy taxes only when it interfered with imports and exports, Hopkinson said. "Here, then, is the whole restriction . . . attempted to be imposed by the constitution, on the power of the States to raise revenue . . . ; and it never was understood by those who made, or those who received the constitution, that any further restriction ever would, or could, be imposed," the lawyer told the Court.

To bolster his argument further, Hopkinson quoted from *The Federalist Papers*, which he called "the great champion of the constitution." Except in the case of imports and exports, *The Federalist Papers* assured readers that the States held a sacred and inviolable right of taxation and "an attempt on the part of the national government to abridge them in the exercise of it, would be a violent assumption of power, unwarranted by any article of clause of its constitution." In addition, he noted, *The Federalist Papers* assured states that they would be "coequals" with the federal government in the matter of taxation.

If the federal bank could not survive if states taxed it, then, contended Hopkinson, the bank should shut down. "For if it can live only by the destruction of such a right—if it can live only by the exercise of a power . . . declared to be a 'violent assumption of power, unwarranted by any article of clause of its constitution'—we cannot hesitate to say, let it not live." But, he quickly added, the state had not sought the destruction of the bank; only the right to regulate it as it would any other corporation. "Its profits will be diminished by contributing to the revenue of the State; and this is the whole effect that ought, in a fair and liberal spirit of reasoning, to be anticipated," the lawyer asserted.

The progression from creation of a federal bank to its expansion into branches that could overrule states' rights was more than a little alarming, Hopkinson told the Court. He compared the bank's growth to that of India's fig trees, whose branches produced new trees until the vegetation covered "a vast surface," killing all other plants in its "spreading shade."

The federal government, Hopkinson noted, relied on only one argument—that "a right to tax is a right to destroy." Fear that the state would abuse its power to destroy the bank, or drive it from its territory, had little basis, he argued. The union of states relied on mutual trust, among states and between states and the federal government. "If the two governments [state and federal] are to regard each other as enemies, seeking opportunities of injury and distress," Hopkinson remarked, "they will not long continue friends." And, he noted sardonically, if the federal government could not trust the state, why should the state trust the federal government?

Furthermore, he argued, states' rights could not be overridden merely because they might violate the obligations of a contract. Section ten of the first article of the Constitution bars states from passing laws "impairing

no state shall . . .

U.S. Constitution, Article I, Section 10. No state shall enter into any treaty, alliance, or confederation; grant letters of marque and reprisal; coin money; emit bills of credit; make anything but gold and silver coin a tender in payment of debts; pass any bill of attainder, ex post facto law, or law impairing the obligation of contracts, or grant any title of nobility.

No state shall, without the consent of the Congress, lay any imposts or duties on imports or exports, except what may be absolutely necessary for executing its inspection laws: and the net produce of all duties and imposts, laid by any state on imports or exports, shall be for the use of the treasury of the United States; and all such laws shall be subject to the revision and control of the Congress.

No state shall, without the consent of Congress, lay any duty of tonnage, keep troops, or ships of war in time of peace, enter into any agreement or compact with another state, or with a foreign power, or engage in war, unless actually invaded, or in such imminent danger as will not admit of delay.

the obligation of contracts." If that applied in this case, the lawyer asserted, "the United States might contract away every right of every State." The federal government itself taxed state banks, he noted, and that had never been considered a violation of a contract. His points made, Hopkinson ended his pleadings and took his seat.

THE GOVERNMENT'S CASE

Next before the Court, U.S. Attorney General William Wirt resumed the argument on behalf of the bank and the federal government. Wirt focused on four points:

> • The power of Congress to create a federal bank had been well established and should not be questioned thirty years later.
> • The Constitution granted Congress the power to do what was necessary to fulfill its duties, and creation of a bank fell within that guarantee.
> • Congress rightfully created the bank and authorized its operation, and that included setting up branches in the states.
> • A law of the United States, passed under the Constitution's requirements, became the supreme law of the land, overriding state laws that disagreed with it.

Wirt noted the length of time that had passed since the first federal bank was set up and the number of laws and court rulings that had upheld the bank's existence during that time. That was proof, he said, that Congress's power to create a federal bank had been "ratified by the voice of the people, and sanctioned by precedent."

In making his second point, he expanded upon Webster's comments. It would make no sense, he said, for the Constitution to give Congress certain powers but not allow it any way to exercise those powers. "A power without the means to use it, is a nullity," Wirt told the Court. The Constitution, he noted, allowed Congress "to make all laws which shall be necessary and proper for carrying into execution" its powers. Establishing a federal bank enabled Congress to carry out several of its powers, the attorney general said. Those included levying and collection taxes, paying off public debts, borrowing money, regulating trade with foreign countries and between states, funding military operations, and waging war.

Requiring Congress to prove that each law passed was *indispensably* necessary would stymie every action the government hoped to take, he said. Congress would never be able to meet such a strict interpretation of the Constitution, since someone could always propose a different law that might accomplish the same purpose. Under that scenario, every law proposed would be rendered unconstitutional, and the restriction would "annihilate the very powers [the Constitution] professes to create," Wirt asserted. He noted that such a requirement would also undermine the nation's existing laws. They could become unconstitutional if circumstances changed. "But surely the constitutionality of any act of Congress cannot depend upon such circumstances," Wirt said. The nation's laws—and Congress's powers to pass them—must have a permanent basis, he argued.

Wirt noted that it was up to Congress—not the courts—to consider Maryland's suggestion of using state banks. That was just another method of accomplishing Congress's goals, and it fell to Congress to decide how best to do that. As it turned out, Congress decided to form a corporation (the federal bank) as the means to accomplish its goals. The founders did not list in the Constitution every means Congress could use to exercise its powers because it would have been impossible to include them all. As a protection against abuse of power, the Court was assigned the job of making sure that the methods used were appropriate and actually linked to the power under which they were set in motion. If a government used methods to accomplish something else—while pretending the methods were necessary to execute a legitimate goal—then the court system could uncover that and put a stop to it. But, Wirt contended, the Court could not legitimately second-guess Congress on which method to use to achieve a constitutional goal.

The same constitutional guarantees applied to all parts of the plan, from the creation of the federal bank to the setting up of state branches, according to the attorney general. "The right, then, to establish these branches, is a necessary part of the means," he told the justices. The bank officers attended to the details of operation, but the branches were authorized by Congress as part of the overall plan, he said.

Making his final point, Wirt disputed Maryland's right to tax the federal bank. The state tax, he concluded, interfered with the bank's operation. Under the sixth article of the Constitution, a federal law was "the supreme law of the land." States were thus barred from passing laws that were contrary to federal statutes, according to Wirt. If the state of Maryland were allowed to interfere with the bank or control it in any way, Wirt said, the state could prevent Congress from exercising the constitutional powers the bank was designed to accomplish. Furthermore, if the state triumphed in the case of the bank, it could tax or otherwise control other federal functions, Wirt claimed. "If this power really exists in the States, its natural and direct tendency is to annihilate any power which belongs to Congress," he said. "But surely, the framers of the constitution did not intend that the exercise of all the powers of the national government should depend upon the discretion of the State governments."

CHANGING THE WHOLE SCHEME
OF GOVERNMENT

At the conclusion of Wirt's arguments, Walter Jones rose to add his support to Maryland's claims. Of all the luminaries in the lineup, Jones had the most experience before the nation's high court. Calling the Constitution a "compact between the States," he reiterated the state's position that "all the powers which are not expressly relinquished by it, are reserved to the States." He firmly rejected the federal government's claim that the federal bank was created merely as a means to enable the United States to levy and collect taxes and duties specified in the Constitution. "It is a commercial institution, a partnership incorporated for the purpose of carrying on the trade of banking," he told the Court.

Jones argued that Congress should be limited to methods "specifically enumerated in the constitution" or related means "naturally connected with the specific means." For example, he noted that Congress could legitimately set up a mint to fulfill its constitutional power to coin money. But setting up a mint, which had to be done in order to coin money, was a far cry from establishing a federal bank. The Constitution, in granting Congress the power to coin money, Jones contended, did "not imply the power of establishing a great banking corporation, branching out into every district of the country, and inundating it with a flood of paper money." To expand Congress's powers in such a way, Jones warned, would "change the whole scheme and theory of the government."

The American people, Jones said, ratified the Constitution reluctantly, and only after being assured that the federal government's power would be "limited to the literal terms" stated in the Constitution. The tenth article provided added assurances that the states would retain all power not specifically set aside for the federal government.

"It would seem that human language could not furnish words less liable to misconstruction!" Jones declared. Yet, he noted, the advocates for the government were trying to use those same words to enlarge federal powers "to an indefinite extent." The Constitution's requirement that the means used to exercise Congress's powers be both "necessary and proper" meant, in Jones's view, that the actions must be "indispensably requisite." Any other meaning, according to the lawyer, would remove the limits placed on governmental powers that the Constitution was designed to ensure.

That said, Jones asked if the federal bank could be considered indispensably requisite for Congress to execute its powers. The answer, he told the justices, was no. "The people never intended [the federal government] should become bankers or traders of any description," Jones said. "They meant to leave to the States the power of regulating the trade of banking, and every other species of internal industry." States were to regulate banks or leave the industry to regulate itself, the lawyer stated. "In either case, Congress would have nothing to do with the subject."

If the government claimed the power to set up banks in the states, Jones cautioned, then it could use the same claims to "establish great trading monopolies, or to lock up the property of the country in [corporations]" by citing "some strained connection between the exercise of such powers, and those expressly given to the government."

The lawyer also attacked the "radical vice" of the federal government's argument that Maryland and other states could not tax the bank. With the exception of the few categories already cited, the states' "power of taxation is absolutely unlimited," Jones declared. "Their power to tax the property of this corporation cannot be denied, without at the same time denying their right to tax any property of the United States." The Constitution, he noted, allowed states to tax U.S. property as long as it did not involve exports and imports. In many cases, he noted, both state and federal government collected taxes on the same entity.

A Final Argument For Maryland

Luther Martin, Maryland's attorney general, rose to make a final pitch for his state and states' rights. A forceful speaker, Martin began his oration on Friday, February 26, and continued through Saturday.

Martin devoted the first part of his arguments to reading from *The Federalist Papers* and the debates of the Constitutional conventions of New York and Virginia. The latter featured the words of a young John Marshall, one of Virginia's delegates taking part in the discussions over the proposed Constitution. Attempting to show that the founders intended to place strict limits on the government's powers, Martin promised to use the chief justice's words to prove his point.

During Martin's recitation, the chief justice appeared uneasy, according to Justice Story. Story noted that Marshall told him later that he was relieved when the lawyer stopped quoting his speeches. "Why, to tell you the truth," the chief justice acknowledged, "I was afraid I had said some foolish things in the debate; but it was not so bad as I expected."

Like Maryland's other advocates, Martin argued that "the framers of the constitution intended to leave nothing to implication." He noted that the Constitution specifically outlined the steps Congress could take in order to wage war: raise and support armies, maintain a navy, and call forth the militia to enforce the nation's laws, among other actions. In that case, Martin asserted, nothing was implied. Therefore, he argued, no additional powers

MARYLAND ATTORNEY GENERAL LUTHER MARTIN DELIVERED THE FINAL ARGUMENTS FOR STATES' RIGHTS IN THE BANK CASE.

should be implied in Congress's financial dealings. "The only safe rule," the attorney general insisted, "is the plain letter of the constitution; . . . that the powers not delegated to the United States, nor prohibited to the States, are reserved to the States respectively, or to the people."

But even if Congress had the right to incorporate a federal bank, Martin claimed it was the right of the state to tax it. Touching again on the words of Daniel Webster, that the power to tax could become the power to destroy, the state's advocate noted, as Hopkinson had, that the federal government could also be tempted by the same abuses.

Concluding his oration, Martin returned to his opening remarks and his understanding of the founders' limits on government power. "The States would not have adopted the constitution," he asserted, if their right to tax had been limited beyond imports and exports.

"Frail and Tottering Edifice" or "Competent Guardian"

The illustrious William Pinkney gave the final speech in the case. As senior counsel for the federal bank, he argued for that institution, but his words served to bolster the federal government's position as well. Beginning on Monday, March 1, Pinkney spoke for three days on the matter. Acknowledged as the leader of the American bar, he spoke with passion and eloquence.

His opening remarks set the tone for the speech, a polished, impassioned soliloquy on the importance of the case. Observers, including at least one justice, would later say the performance was Pinkney's greatest. He began:

> I meditate with exultation, not fear, upon
> the proud spectacle of a peaceful review of
> these conflicting sovereign claims by this
> . . . Council. I see in it a pledge of the

immortality of the Union, of a perpetuity of national strength and glory, increasing and brightening with age: —of concord at home and reputation abroad.

In the hushed courtroom, Pinkney continued, noting that the Court's decision in the case would extend far beyond the fate of a bank; it could determine the very survival of the Constitution and the democratic government it had established:

> I ascribe to the judgment that may be pronounced in this case a mighty, a gigantic influence, that will travel down to the latest posterity, and give shape and character to the destinies of this republican empire.

> It is not merely that it may stabilitate or pull down a financial or commercial institution called a Bank—however essential such an institution may be to the government and country. I have a deep and awful conviction . . . that upon that judgment it will mainly depend whether the constitution under which we live and prosper is to be considered, like its precursor, a mere phantom of political power to deceive and mock us—a pageant of mimic sovereignty calculated to raise up hopes that it may leave them to perish — a frail and tottering edifice, that can afford no shelter from storms either foreign or domestic—a creature half made up, without a heart or brain, or nerve or muscle—without protecting power or redeeming energy—or whether it

> is to be viewed as a competent guardian of
> all that is dear to us as a nation.

Getting down to business, Pinkney deftly dispatched the constitutional question. Members of the audience, who had waited days to hear the prestigious lawyer, followed each word.

First, Pinkney dismissed comparisons between the Constitution and the confederation, which he said were as different "as light from darkness." The confederation—"a mere federative league" formed by the states to fight the Revolution—had no power except what it attained through force. The Constitution, on the other hand, sprang not from the states, but directly from the people. The people, too, vested the federal government with its authority, according to Pinkney.

The constitutionality of a federal bank had long been settled, he said. In fact the framers of the Constitution themselves had been leaders in the Congress that approved the first federal bank. "They must have understood their own work," he declared. The power of Congress to establish the bank did not need to be "expressed in the text of the constitution," Pinkney contended; "it might safely be left to implication."

Subsequent acts of Congress, he said, similarly confirmed the authority to create a federal bank. Congress went through the usual process to establish the second federal bank. Opponents and proponents discussed the bill's pros and cons, and in 1816 voted in favor of the bank's establishment. "Congress is . . . a competent judge of its own constitutional powers," Pinkney contended. "It is not . . . the exclusive judge," he acknowledged, but noted that Congress did review bills for constitutionality before passing them. And in all the discussion of the bank, he noted, the constitutionality of the legislation creating the

THE ELOQUENT WILLIAM PINKNEY GAVE FINAL ARGUMENTS IN THE CASE ON BEHALF OF THE NATIONAL BANK.

corporation never became an issue. Likewise, the courts had upheld the legality of the bank, he said.

Pinkney maintained that the Constitution gave Congress the tools to do its job. "All the objects of the government are national objects, and the means are, and must be, fitted to accomplish them." Pinkney proceeded to list the vitally important goals of the national government—establish justice, insure domestic tranquility, provide for the common defense, promote the general welfare, secure the blessings of liberty. Yet with all this important work to be done, Pinkney marveled, some would doubt that the government had the authority to create a corporation to help accomplish the tasks. Even individual states, he noted, had the authority to create corporations even though such power was not mentioned in the state constitution.

Pinkney expanded on Wirt's discussion of the need for implied powers. To list all the methods to be used to accomplish Congress's goals, the framers of the Constitution would have had to include "an immense variety of details," he said. And even then, the chore would be impossible because they would not be able to foresee "the infinite variety of circumstances" in a society "forever changing and forever improving."

He discarded Martin's notion that each method Congress used to further the national goals had to be "indispensably necessary." For example, he noted that Congress established light houses, beacons, buoys, and public piers "under the general power to regulate commerce." But, he added, "they are not indispensably necessary to commerce. It might linger on without those aids, though exposed to more perils and losses." Certainly, he acknowledged, Congress's action had to be appropriate; there had to be a relationship between the means used and the end accomplished. As long as those conditions were met, however, the choice of which method to use belonged to Congress, Pinkney argued. The Court, he contended, could not rightfully come back and say another method was better or more necessary.

Next Pinkney explored whether the federal bank actually furthered the goals of the nation. It did, he concluded, in several ways by:

- transferring funds of the government where directed;
- issuing notes that could be used to pay off debts;
- enabling the government to borrow money;
- involvement in the financial operations of the government;
- facilitating foreign and interstate commerce; and
- providing a currency used in trade.

The state banks could provide some but not all of those services, he noted, but that did not reduce the federal bank's usefulness. The power to establish the bank's branches came from the same source that allowed creation of the parent bank, he said. The branches, he contended, were "Identical with the parent bank."

Finally, Pinkney considered Maryland's claim that it should be entitled to tax the federal bank. The consequence of granting states the right to tax the bank could well lead to the destruction of the institution, the lawyer said. "Whatever the United States have a right to do," he noted, "the individual States have no right to undo." Echoing Daniel Webster's statement, he declared, "A right to tax without limit or control, is essentially a power to destroy." And that power could be used against other federal entities as well, he said.

He cautioned the Court against allowing states to tax federal entities under certain conditions. The Court would have no way to tell for sure the intent behind the tax and the ultimate effect it might have on an institution, the lawyer said. "The legislative intention may be so masked," he warned, "as to defy the scrutinizing eye of the Court." If the Court allowed the Maryland tax, he said, it would then have to decide whether to approve a similar tax imposed by Kentucky. Could the bank survive a tax of sixty thousand dollars per year? Pinkney asked the justices. "*Probably* it could not; but judicial *certainty* is essential; and the Court has no means of arriving at that certainty," Pinkney said.

Noting that states were barred from taxing foreign vessels that came to port, Pinkney asked should not the same protection apply "for the security of our own government?"

The lawyer argued that the branch bank in Maryland and the Circuit Court of Maryland both were instruments of the national government; both were created to serve the goals of the United States; and both should have an equal claim for immunity from state taxes. Yet states did not tax the federal court system, even though the Constitution did not specifically prohibit it. The exemption arose from "the general nature of the government, and from the principle of the supremacy of the national powers, and the laws made to execute them, over the State authorities and State laws," Pinkney said. Such principles, he argued, should also cover the bank's situation.

After holding the Court's attention for three days, the great orator concluded his speech with a strong argument for a "fair and liberal interpretation" of the government's constitutional powers and urged the Court to rule in the bank's favor. "No other alternative remains," Pinkney told the justices, "but for this court to interpose its authority, and save the nation from the consequences of this dangerous attempt."

Pinkney's eloquence, his mastery of the law, and his

ability to grasp the complex issues involved and simplify them for his audience had great influence on the Court. Justice Story wrote about the speech in awe:

> I never, in my whole life, heard a greater speech; it was worth a journey from Salem to hear it; his elocution was excessively vehement, but his eloquence was overwhelming. His language, his style, his figures, his arguments were most brilliant and sparkling. He spoke like a great statesman and a patriot, and a sound constitutional lawyer. All the cobwebs of sophistry and metaphysics about States' rights and State Sovereignty he brushed away with a mighty besom [broom].

FIVE
THE DECISION

ON MARCH 6, 1819, only three days after Pinkney's extraordinary performance, Chief Justice John Marshall issued the decision he had written for a unanimous court. Far from the narrow verdict on a bank tax that it could have been, the sweeping decision reinforced the supremacy of the national government over the states.

From his first statement, Marshall made it clear that the opinion would address the larger constitutional question pitting the powers of the federal government against those of individual states. The decision would be among the Court's most important, he knew, since it could "essentially influence the great operations of the government." Predicting accurately the storm that would consume the nation in a civil war forty years later, the chief justice warned that the issue "must be decided peacefully" by the Court or it would become the source "of hostility of a still more serious nature."

Marshall first addressed whether Congress had the power to incorporate a federal bank. He gave weight to the actions of the past: the first Congress's approval of a federal bank, laws establishing the bank, and court rulings that upheld its creation. But, he noted, even if the first bank had not been established, the Constitution itself would uphold the incorporation.

CHIEF JUSTICE JOHN MARSHALL DELIVERED THE UNANIMOUS RULING IN
THE BANK CASE ON MARCH 6, 1819. THAT OPINION, WHICH ESTABLISHED THE
POWER OF THE FEDERAL GOVERNMENT OVER INDIVIDUAL STATES, HELPED
DETERMINE HOW THE UNITED STATES WOULD BE GOVERNED.

At the heart of the disagreement over the Constitution's interpretation lay two views of that document's origins, according to Marshall. Maryland contended that the Constitution came about as the result of a compact among "sovereign and independent States." According to this view, the states alone had "supreme dominion." They delegated powers to the national government, which remained subordinate to the individual states.

Marshall discarded this proposition. He acknowledged that state legislatures had elected those who participated in the convention which drafted the Constitution. But it was the people who met in conventions in each state and who ultimately approved the document. "The instrument was submitted to the people [and] they acted upon it . . . by assembling in convention," Marshall wrote. The chief justice noted that the people held their conventions in their own states, but that did not mean the measures they adopted "cease to be the measures of the people themselves, or become the measures of the State governments."

power Beyond the state

This second view of the Constitution's origins—that it derived from the people—gave it power beyond that of the states, Marshall said.

> The government proceeds directly from the people; is "ordained and established" in the name of the people; and is declared to be ordained, "in order to form a more perfect union, establish justice, ensure domestic tranquility, and secure the blessings of liberty to themselves and to their posterity." The assent of the States, in their sovereign capacity, is implied in calling a convention, and thus submitting that

> instrument to the people. But the people
> were at perfect liberty to accept or reject it;
> and their act was final. It required not the
> affirmance, and could not be negatived, by
> the State governments. The constitution,
> when thus adopted, was of complete obli-
> gation, and bound the State sovereignties
> ... [and] is, emphatically, and truly, a gov-
> ernment of the people.

That the Constitution limited the powers of the federal
government had been well established, Marshall said. The
perpetual controversy, which he correctly predicted
"would probably continue to arise as long as our system
shall exist," focused on the extent of the powers that had
been granted. The chief justice acknowledged that the
Constitution did not list the establishment of a bank
among the powers specifically granted the federal government. But he noted the Constitution also did not specify
that implied powers were not allowed. Listing every means
by which to carry out each power would have turned the
Constitution into a legal code, complex and lengthy, Marshall said. "It would probably never be understood by the
public."

Instead, Marshall said, the framers used broad strokes
to draw up their document, an outline with only the
important parts designated. The rest—"minor ingredi-
ents"—could be deduced from the document itself. "In
considering this question, then," Marshall reminded his
audience, "we must never forget that it is a constitution we
are expounding."

The chief justice firmly rejected the notion that the federal government —by way of its vastness and power—could
legitimately gobble up smaller powers. But a government
entrusted with such powers, he reasoned, should also be

trusted to use the means to carry out its objectives. The Constitution did not bar Congress from creating a corporation, if that helped accomplish its goals. "The government which has a right to do an act, and has imposed on it the duty of performing that act, must, according to the dictates of reason, be allowed to select the means," Marshall wrote.

The power to create a corporation, he noted, was far different from the power to wage war. The first was a tool, the latter a "great substantive and independent power," according to the opinion. Calling the formation of a corporation a "power" was not "sufficient reason" to bar Congress from using that tool to achieve its ends, Marshall wrote.

The chief justice let the Constitution speak for itself in his argument for a liberal interpretation of the document. In the opinion, Marshall explored the meaning of the words "necessary and proper" when referring to congressional actions allowed under the Constitution. If the framers of the Constitution had intended to restrict Congress's acts only to those listed, he argued, they would have required that federal laws and actions be "absolutely necessary," a term used elsewhere in the document.

The men who drew up the Constitution, Marshall reflected, intended for it "to endure for ages to come." Knowing they could not foresee future crises the nation would face, the framers created a document that could adapt to whatever arose. The chief justice noted: "It would have been an unwise attempt to provide, by immutable rules, for exigencies which, if foreseen at all, must have been seen dimly, and which can be best provided for as they occur." To limit Congress to a short list of acceptable courses of action, Marshall said, "would have been to deprive the legislature of the capacity to avail itself of experience, to exercise its reason, and to accommodate its legislation to circumstances."

More than a "splendid bauble," the Constitution was a

THE SUPREME COURT MOVED INTO NEWLY DESIGNED QUARTERS IN THE BASE-
MENT OF THE SENATE CHAMBERS IN FEBRUARY 1819, JUST IN TIME TO HEAR

ARGUMENTS IN THE *McCulloch* CASE.

sound document that allowed Congress to use its discretion in picking appropriate methods to do its job. But it also provided ways to stop Congress from abusing its power, Marshall assured. That, he noted, became the Court's responsibility. "Should Congress, under the pretext of executing its powers, pass laws for the accomplishment of objects not entrusted to the government; it would become the painful duty of this tribunal, should a case requiring such a decision come before it, to say that such an act was not the law of the land."

It was not the Court's role, however, to second-guess Congress in its decisions on how to accomplish legitimate goals, Marshall said. "This court disclaims all pretensions to such a power." To allow the states that power, he added, "would render [national] course precarious, the result of its measures uncertain, and create a dependence on other governments, which might disappoint its most important designs, and is incompatible with the language of the constitution." Therefore, Marshall declared, the Court had decided unanimously "that the act to incorporate the Bank of the United States is a law made in pursuance of the constitution, and is a part of the supreme law of the land."

National Powers Supreme

The chief justice devoted the second half of the opinion to the issue of whether Maryland had the right to tax the bank's branch. He acknowledged that the Constitution gave the states the power of taxation, and that it was of "vital importance" to the states. But, he argued, the Constitution limited even that right when it interfered with other constitutional actions, such as importing and exporting goods.

Here Marshall delivered the doctrine that would influence all future states' rights controversies and set the course of American law for generations: *The Constitution* and the federal laws made under it were supreme; they controlled the laws and constitutions of the states and could not be controlled by them.

That principle, Marshall said, pervaded the Constitution, was "interwoven with its web," and was "blended with its texture." National supremacy could not be removed from the Constitution, the chief justice asserted, "without rending it into shreds."

He used this principle to bar the states from taxing federal property. Because national laws ruled supreme, Marshall said, state laws could not override them or be used to interfere with national purposes. Agreeing with the bank's lawyers that taxation could be used as a tool of destruction, he ruled that Maryland's tax on the federal bank could not be allowed. States' sovereignty did not extend over institutions created by federal powers, according to Marshall. "Those powers are not given by the people of a single State. They are given by the people of the United States, to a government whose laws, made in pursuance of the constitution, are declared to be supreme. Consequently, the people of a single State cannot confer a sovereignty which will extend over them."

Marshall addressed Maryland's argument that states did not necessarily use taxes to destroy an entity and that the state should be trusted not to abuse its power. Just as one state would not trust another state to tax its property, so one state should not be trusted to tax the property of a federal government acting for all the states, Marshall reasoned. "The legislature of the Union alone, therefore, can be trusted by the people with the power of controlling measures which concern all," he wrote.

Allowing states to tax federal property, the chief justice contended, would put states in control of government operations. They could tax the mail, patent rights, the courts, the mint, and the papers of the custom house;

through taxation, he said, the states could "defeat all the ends of government." That was not the intention of the American people when they enacted the Constitution, according to Marshall. "They did not design to make their government dependent on the States."

The chief justice concluded the opinion with one final declaration of the national government's supremacy: "The States have no power, by taxation or otherwise, to retard, impede, burden, or in any manner control, the operations of the constitutional laws enacted by Congress to carry into execution the powers vested in the general government."

Although some legal experts credit Daniel Webster with convincing the Court to rule as it did, historian Robert M. Ireland makes the case for Pinkney. According to Ireland, Justice Gabriel Duvall's letters reveal that the Court had "very strong doubts" about the stand taken by the bank and the federal government before Pinkney gave his remarkable address. Apparently the lawyer's eloquence removed all doubt, since the Court—with its majority of Republicans—voted unanimously in support of the federal government.

Justice Robert Jackson, who served on the Court from 1941 to 1954, gave Chief Justice John Marshall full due for the extraordinary opinion of the Court. He surmised that Marshall wrote much of his great opinion before the oral arguments began, since it was delivered only three days after the hearing ended. "It was constructed not so much by a judge as by a master statesman," said Jackson. "The opinion was deliberately made as broad as possible; Marshall intended to reach far beyond his court room and to chart a path for the entire nation."

SIX
A NATION IS BORN

THE SUPREME COURT'S DECISION in *McCulloch v. Maryland* represented a major turning point in American history. According to Supreme Court Justice Robert Jackson, "a nation was born in the decision of *McCulloch v. Maryland*." The decision rescued the national government, establishing it as a strong, central union instead of an entity that existed only at the pleasure of all-powerful independent states. The Court's liberal interpretation of the Constitution gave the national government the means to deal with "the various crises of human affairs" forever afterward.

Justice Jackson believed the decision preserved the nation:

> Were it not for the principles of *McCulloch v. Maryland* we hardly could be a nation today, and what we have come to view as legitimate, if not inescapable, national functions may virtually all be traced to the doctrine established by the Court when it rejected Maryland's plea.

The decision immediately became headline news. The *National Intelligencer* in Washington, D.C. reported in its March 13 edition, "The Supreme Judicial authority of the

According to Justice Robert Jackson, who served on the Supreme Court from 1941 to 1954, John Marshall's decision in *McCulloch* v. *Maryland* preserved the nation.

nation has rarely, if ever, pronounced an opinion more interesting in its views or more important in its operation."

"It excites great interest, and in a political view is of the deepest consequence to the nation," Judge Story wrote of the ruling. "It goes to establish the Constitution upon its great original principle."

Sharp divisions formed along party lines as soon as Marshall delivered the opinion. Federalists celebrated the chief justice's sweeping decision. The decision, trumpeted the *Boston Daily Advertiser*, was "one of the most able judgments ever delivered."

Those who favored states' rights, particularly in the South and West, expressed outrage at what they perceived as an infringement of their power as sovereign states. Thomas Jefferson's followers in the Democratic-Republican party denounced it. The *Niles Register*, a Democratic paper in Maryland, bitterly attacked the decision as "a total frustration of the state-rights and the loss of the liberties of the nation." In its March 13 edition, the paper referred to the decision as "a deadly blow . . . struck at the Sovereignty of the States" one which delivered "a dangerous blow" to the welfare of the Union. It issued a dire warning that the decision "may be wielded to destroy the whole revenues and so do away with the Sovereignties of the States."

The *Richmond Enquirer* in Virginia reported similar misgivings about the Court: "If such a spirit as breathes on this opinion is forever to preside over the judiciary, then indeed it is high time for the State to tremble; that in all their great fights may be swept away one by one, that those sovereign States may dwindle into paltry and contemptible corporations."

Though Marshall's opinion may have preserved the Union, it could not quell the political controversy over the bank or states' rights. Virginia's legislature passed a resolution, "a most solemn protest," against the bank. In Ohio, officials forcibly seized money from a branch in lieu of taxes the state claimed the bank owed. After the ruling, a total of forty-one lawsuits were filed against the bank. Daniel Webster defended the bank in those cases argued before the Supreme Court, all of which he won. The bank closed in 1836 after President Andrew Jackson vetoed the renewal of its charter. Jackson and his supporters, like detractors in the past, insisted that the bank threatened democracy by controlling the nation's economy and giving the central government too much power.

The battle over states' rights raged on. Southern states, perceiving that a strong central government might take steps to end slavery, led the battle. States' rights proponents saw the Supreme Court as the enemy in their fight to retain power.

Anger over the Court's decisions limiting states' rights led to efforts in Congress to reduce the Court's power. In 1822, a representative from Virginia introduced a bill to bar the Supreme Court from overruling the final decisions of the states' appeals courts. In another attempt to control the Court, a Kentucky congressman proposed a constitutional amendment that would have allowed the Senate to review appeals that involved states. The following year Senator Richard M. Johnson, a Democratic-Republican from Kentucky, proposed that the Supreme Court be allowed to declare a state law unconstitutional only if seven justices agreed. Congress considered yet another bill in January 1824, this one to repeal the entire section of the Judiciary Act that gave the Supreme Court the authority to hear appeals from state courts involving the constitutionality of state or federal laws. All of the measures failed.

Commenting on the efforts to thwart the Court, Justice Story wrote in 1822 that the judiciary "must always be open

THE DOWNFALL OF MOTHER BANK.

AN 1832 CARTOON SHOWS PRESIDENT ANDREW JACKSON DISCARDING THE
CHARTER AUTHORIZING THE NATIONAL BANK OF THE UNITED STATES.
JACKSON'S WITHDRAWAL OF FEDERAL FUNDS FROM THE BANK CAUSED THE
"DOWNFALL OF MOTHER BANK," AS PORTRAYED BY THE CARTOONIST, AND
THREW THE NATION INTO ECONOMIC CHAOS.

to attack from all quarters. . . . Its only support is the wise
and the good and the elevated in society; and these, as we all
know, must ever remain in a discouraging minority in
all Governments. . . . For the Judges of the Supreme Court
there is but one course to pursue. That is, to do their duty
firmly and honestly, according to their best judgments."

Senator Johnson's proposal drew the ire of Marshall,
who wrote that requiring near unanimity would "require
what cannot often happen." Such a provision, he said,

would "disable the court from deciding constitutional questions."

Later court cases

After the *McCulloch* decision, the Marshall Court issued several other rulings that strengthened the position of the federal government in relation to the states. In the 1821 case of *Cohens* v. *Virginia*, the state convicted the Cohens of selling District of Columbia lottery tickets in Virginia. Congress had authorized the lottery in the District of Columbia, but Virginia state law prohibited it. In addition, Virginia officials declared that they had authority to settle disputes between the state and the federal government. Writing for a united Court, Chief Justice Marshall decreed that the U.S. Supreme Court, not the states, had the final say in constitutional matters, both civil and criminal. State laws and constitutions that violated federal laws or the Constitution, Marshall wrote, were "absolutely void." The decision further cemented the Court's role as final arbiter on the Constitution.

Thomas Jefferson had been a fierce critic of the judiciary ever since the Supreme Court ruled against him in *Marbury* v. *Madison*, the case that established the independence of the judiciary. An outspoken critic of the *McCulloch* decision, he weighed in again after the controversial *Cohens* v. *Virginia*. In a letter, the former president expressed his concern over what he perceived as the Court's abuse of power in supporting a powerful central government and eroding states' rights. "I am sensible of the inroads daily making by the Federal, into the jurisdiction of its co-ordinate associates, the State governments. The legislative and executive branches may sometimes err, but elections and dependence will bring them to rights. The judiciary branch is the instrument which, working like gravity, without intermission, is to press us at last into

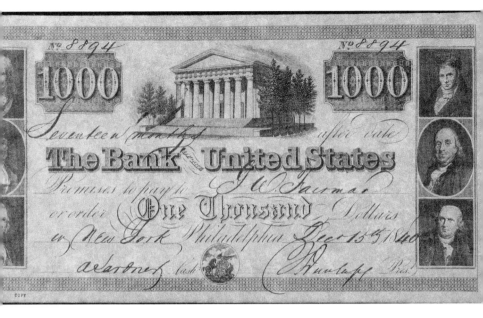

THE PENNSYLVANIA-CHARTERED BANK OF THE UNITED STATES ISSUED
BONDS LIKE THE ONE SHOWN HERE. AFTER THE CHARTER OF THE SECOND
NATIONAL BANK LAPSED, THE BANK CONTINUED TO OPERATE AS A STATE-
CHARTERED BANK. NICHOLAS BIDDLE, WHO HAD SERVED AS PRESIDENT OF
THE NATIONAL BANK, CONTINUED IN THAT POST AS HEAD OF THE STATE BANK.
THE BANK EVENTUALLY FAILED AND CLOSED ITS DOORS IN 1841.

one consolidated mass." He particularly blamed John
Marshall for the Court's support of national supremacy
over the states. "The practice of Judge Marshall of travel-
ling out of his case to prescribe what the law would be in a
moot case not before the court is very irregular and very
censurable," Jefferson wrote.

Jefferson's attacks had little effect on Marshall. He
continued to promote a strong federal government in subsequent cases. In *Gibbons* v. *Ogden*, a landmark case
decided in 1824, the Court—again in a unanimous decision—ruled that Congress could constitutionally control
commerce that affected more than one state. The case

involved a suit by two steamship operators to prevent another operator, Thomas Gibbons, from competing with them. The state of New York had granted the two operators an exclusive contract to ferry passengers between New York and New Jersey. Congress had granted Gibbons a license to serve the same route. In his decision, Marshall relied on the Constitution's Commerce Clause in Article I, Section 8, which gave Congress the power "to regulate Commerce with foreign Nations, and among the several States." He ruled that Congress could legitimately grant the contract; he also expanded the definition of commerce to include navigation and transport between states.

The decisions set precedents that would serve as a base for the rule of law far into the future. They failed, however, in their efforts to quell the bitter dispute over states' rights versus federal power. That controversy reached a boiling point when southern states, in an ultimate move to assert their sovereignty, seceded from the union. It took a Civil War and years of Reconstruction to reestablish the supremacy of the national government.

During the 1950s and 1960s, the Court under Chief Justice Earl Warren used its power to decide the constitutionality of state laws—as established by the Marshall decisions—to expand the individual rights of juveniles, poor defendants, and women, and promote civil rights for black Americans.

The *McCulloch* ruling and the other landmark decisions of the Marshall Court still stand today as established law on which our system is based. Throughout most of the twentieth century, the Court has generally followed the lead of the Marshall Court in accepting the implied powers doctrine stated in *McCulloch*. Court rulings have consistently expanded the powers of the federal government in overseeing a wide variety of problems, from the environment to foreign affairs.

critics' concerns

Critics of the Court, however, believe the doctrine has been stretched too far. They oppose Court rulings in the twentieth century that they believe have allowed Congress to delegate power to federal agencies and the president. In a 1989 case, the Court ruled that the Constitution barred a delegation of power. But, the justices said, Congress could obtain help from the other branches. Writing for the majority in *Mistretta* v. *United States*, Justice Harry Blackmun wrote: "Our jurisprudence has been driven by a practical understanding that in our increasingly complex society, replete with ever changing and more technical problems, Congress simply cannot do its job absent an ability to delegate power under broad general directives."

The critics fear that such decisions have eroded the rights reserved to the states and the people and expanded the powers of the federal government far beyond what the framers intended. "The most serious inroads on the doctrine of enumerated powers are . . . the vast expansion in recent years of national legislative power in the regulation of commerce among the States and in the expenditure of the national revenues," according to one legal expert.

Beginning in 1995, the conservative Court under Chief Justice William H. Rehnquist reflected those concerns in many of its decisions. The Court invalidated a long list of laws and provisions passed by Congress that they believed overreached its authority. Among the acts rejected by the Court were provisions of the Brady Handgun Act, the Religious Freedom Restoration Act, the Gun Free School Zones Act, the Age Discrimination in Employment Act, and the Violence Against Women Act. Unlike the Marshall Court, however, the Court under Rehnquist garnered only a slim 5 to 4 majority in most cases. How the Court under Chief Justice John Roberts will rule on upcoming cases remains to be seen.

UNDER CHIEF JUSTICE WILLIAM H. REHNQUIST, THE U.S. SUPREME COURT
OVERRODE SEVERAL LAWS PASSED BY CONGRESS IN FAVOR OF STATES' RIGHTS.

112

Whatever course the Supreme Court follows, it will forever be indebted to Chief Justice John Marshall for winning respect for the judiciary. Without such respect, the Court's decisions would have little impact. Even when they disagree violently with Court decisions, citizens and states eventually obey the rulings. For example, the *Brown v. Board of Education* decisions elicited bitter resistance, but states eventually desegregated their schools. As Justice Tom Clark, who served on the Court from 1949 to 1967, once said, "You know, we don't have money at the Court for an army, and we can't take ads in the newspapers, and we don't want to go out on a picket line in our robes. We have to convince the nation by the force of our opinions."

NOTES

Introduction

p. 9, par. 3, Robert H. Jackson, "Maryland at the Supreme Court," Maryland State Bar Association, 44 Md. S.B.A. Proc. III (1939).

p. 9, par. 3, *McCulloch* v. *Maryland*, 4 Wheaton 316 (1819).

Chapter 1

p. 17, par. 1, Clinton Rossiter, *Alexander Hamilton and the Constitution*. New York: Harcourt, Brace & World, Inc., 1964, 40.

p. 18, par. 3, *The Federalist Papers*, University of Oklahoma College of Law. http://www.law.ou.edu/hist/federalist

Sidebar

p. 19, U.S. Constitution, article X.

p. 19, par. 1, Rossiter, *Alexander Hamilton and the Constitution*, 78, note.

p. 19, par. 2, Thomas Jefferson to James Madison, 1787, *The Papers of Thomas Jefferson*, 12:440, University of Virginia, 6:388. http://etext.virginia.edu/jefferson/quotations/jeff0950.htm

p. 21, par. 1, Rossiter, *Alexander Hamilton and the Constitution*, 200.

p. 21, par. 3, National Park Service, "First Bank of the United States," The U.S. Constitution. http://www.cr .nps.gov/history/online_books/butowsky2/ constitution5.htm

Sidebar
p. 24–25, U.S. Constitution, article I, sec. 8.

p. 28, par. 1, Thomas Jefferson, "Jefferson's Opinion on the Constitutionality of a National Bank, 1791." The Avalon Project at Yale Law School. http://www.yale. edu/lawweb/avalon/amerdoc/bank-tj.htm

p. 29, par. 3, Alexander Hamilton, "Hamilton's Opinion as to the Constitutionality of the Bank of the United States, 1791." The Avalon Project at Yale Law School. http://www.yale.edu/lawweb/avalon/amerdoc/ bank-tj.htm

Chapter 2
p. 33, par. 3, David Cowen, "The First Bank of the United States." EH.net Encyclopedia. http://eh.net/ encyclopedia/article/cowen.banking.first_bank.us

Sidebar
p. 36–38, The Supreme Court Historical Society. http://www.supremecourthistory.org Administrative Office of the U.S. Courts. http://www.uscourts.gov Iowa Court Information System. http://www.judicial.state.ia.us/students/6 There is also a diagram on the last Web site.

p. 39, par. 4, "*Sturges* v. *Crowninshield* (4 Wheaton 122 (1819))," *Great Cases in the Classroom*, Boston Partners in Education. http://bostonpartners.org/programs/

index.cfm?ac=greatcases8th

p. 41, par. 1, *Sturges* v. *Crowninshield*, 4 Wheaton 122 (1819).

p. 41, par. 2, Edward S. Corwin, *John Marshall and the Constitution*, The Library of American Freedoms. Richmond, IN: Palladium Press, 2004, 14.

Chapter 3

p. 44, par. 2, William H. Rehnquist, "John Marshall" (remarks, College of William and Mary, Williamsburg, VA, October 6, 2000).

p. 45, par. 1, G. Edward White, "Imagining the Marshall Court," *Supreme Court Historical Society 1986 Yearbook*, digital collection from the Supreme Court Historical Society.

http://www.supremecourthistory.org/04_library/subs _volumes/04_c18_m.html

Sidebar

p. 46–47, Douglas O. Linder, "Justice Joseph Story," in *Famous American Trials: Amistad Trials*, University of Missouri School of Law Web site, 1998. http://www .law.umkc.edu/faculty/projects/ftrials/amistad/ami _bsto.htm

Pennsylvania Avenue National Historic Park Web site. http://www.nps.gov/paav/hotels.htm

Sarah Luria, "National Domesticity in the Early Republic: Washington, D.C.," *Common-Place*, 3, no. 4 (July 2003). http://www.common-place.org/vol-03/ no-04/washington

Dacor Bacon House Foundation, "The History of the Dacor Bacon House," Dacor Bacon House Foundation Web site. http://www.dacorbacon.org/DBHF/Dacor _Bacon_House.htm

p. 48, par. 1, Library of Virginia, "John Marshall," an exhibition at the Library of Virginia, January 8, 2001–March 31, 2001. http://www.lva.lib.va.us/ whoweare/exhibits/marshall/index.htm

p. 48, par. 1, Rehnquist, "John Marshall."

p. 49, par. 3, White, "Imagining the Marshall Court."

p. 50, par. 1, White, "Imagining the Marshall Court."

p. 50, par. 1, John Paul Jones, "Gabriel Duvall," in the OYEZ Project, http://www.oyez.org/justices/ gabriel_duvall

p. 50, par. 2, White, "Imagining the Marshall Court."

p. 50, par. 2, "Brockholst Livingston," in the OYEZ Project, http://www.oyez.org/justices/brockholst _livingston

p. 51, par. 2, "Bushrod Washington," in the OYEZ Project, http://www.oyez.org/justices/bushrod_washington

p. 52, par. 1, G. Edward White, "Imagining the Marshall Court."

p. 52, par. 2, Supreme Court Historical Society, "The Marshall Court, 1801–1835," *History of the Court.* http://www.supremecourthistory.org/02_history/subs _history/02_c04.html

p. 54, par. 1, Calvin Lane, "Joseph Story, Associate Justice, U.S. Supreme Court," Exploring Amistad at Mystic Seaport Web site. http://amistad.mystic seaport.org/discovery/people/bio.story.joseph.html

p. 54, par. 3–p. 55, par. 1, Rex E. Lee, "Remarks on the Bicentennial of the Supreme Court," *Supreme Court Historical Society 1990 Yearbook*, digital collection from the Supreme Court Historical Society. http://www .supremecourthistory.org/04_library/subs_volumes/ 04c_12_e.html

p. 55, par. 2, Supreme Court Historical Society, "The Marshall Court, 1801–1835," *History of the Court.* http://www.supremecourthistory.org/02_history/sub _history/02_c04.html

p. 56, par. 1, John F. Kennedy, *Profiles in Courage*. New York: Harper Perennial Modern Classics, 2004, 58.

p. 56, par. 4, Joseph C. Robert, "The Many-Sided Attorney General," *Supreme Court Historical Society 1976 Yearbook*, digital collection from the Supreme Court Historical Society. http://www.supremecourt history.org/04_library/subs_volumes/04_co1_g.html

p. 56, par. 4, William Draper Lewis, ed. *Great American Lawyers*, vol. 2. Philadelphia: The John C. Winston Company, 1907, 177.

p. 57, par. 1, John B. Boles, *A Guide to the Microfilm Edition of the William Wirt Papers, 1784–1864*. Baltimore: Maryland Historical Society, 1971.

p. 57, par. 1, Robert, "The Many-Sided Attorney General."

p. 57, par. 1, Lewis, ed. *Great American Lawyers*, 309.

p. 57, par. 2, Robert M. Ireland, "William Pinkney: A Revision and Re-emphasis," *American Journal of Legal History* 14, no. 3 (July 1970), 235-246.

p. 57, par. 2, Stephen M. Shapiro, "The Supreme Court's Greatest Advocate," Supreme Court and Appellate Practice Group Web site. http://www.appellate.net/ articles/wilpin799.asp

p. 58, par. 1, Samuel Tyler, *Memoir of Roger Brooke Taney: Chief Justice of the Supreme Court of the United States*. Baltimore: J. Murphy & Company, 1872, 69, cited in Lewis, *Great American Lawyers*, 216–219.

p. 58, par. 2, Lewis, *Great American Lawyers*, 177–178.

p. 58, par. 2, William Pinkney Whyte, "William Pinkney" (address, Maryland State Bar Association, 1904, 86) cited in Lewis, *Great American Lawyers*, 178.

p. 59, par. 1, Lewis, *Great American Lawyers*, 16.

p. 59, par. 2, Lewis, *Great American Lawyers*, 20–24.

p. 60, par. 3, Shapiro, "The Supreme Court's Greatest Advocate."

p. 60, par. 3, Maurice Glen Baxter, *Daniel Webster and the*

Supreme Court. Amherst, MA: University of Massachusetts Press, 1966, 30.

p. 61, par. 1, Joseph Packard, "General Walter Jones," *Virginia Law Register* 7, no. 4 (August 1901).

Chapter 4

p. 63, par. 3, Rex E. Lee, "Remarks on the Bicentennial of the Supreme Court," *Supreme Court Historical Society 1990 Yearbook*, digital collection from the Supreme Court Historical Society. http://www.supremecourt history.org/04_library/subs_volumes/04_c12_e.html

p. 64, par. 1, Harvey H. Miller, "The Supreme Court As A Nation Builder," paper presented at American College of Bankruptcy Induction Ceremony, March 18, 2005.

p. 64, par. 3, *National Intelligencer* (February 25, 1819), cited in "The Federal Bar and the Law, 1815–1830," *The Informer*, http://www.atgpress.com/inform/ ab013.htm

Sidebar

p. 65–66, Philip B. Kurland and Gerhard Casper, eds. *Landmark Briefs and Arguments of the Supreme Court of the United States: Constitutional Law*, preface to vols. 1–4. Washington, DC: University Publications of America Inc., 1, 1978.

p. 67, par. 1–p. 70, par. 2, Daniel Webster, oral arguments, *McCulloch* v. *Maryland*, 4 Wheaton 316 (1819). Printed in *Landmark Briefs and Arguments of the Supreme Court of the United States: Constitutional Law*, 322–330.

p. 72, par. 2–p. 76, par. 4; p. 78, par. 1, Joseph Hopkinson, oral arguments, *McCulloch* v. *Maryland*, 4 Wheaton 316 (1819). Printed in *Landmark Briefs and Arguments of the Supreme Court of the United States: Constitutional Law*, 330–352.

Sidebar

p. 77, U.S. Constitution, article I, sec. 10.

p. 78, par. 4–p. 80, par. 3, William Wirt, oral arguments, *McCulloch v. Maryland*, 4 Wheaton 316 (1819). Printed in *Landmark Briefs and Arguments of the Supreme Court of the United States: Constitutional Law*, 352–362.

p. 81, par. 1–p. 82, par. 1, Walter Jones, oral arguments, *McCulloch v. Maryland*, 4 Wheaton 316 (1819). Printed in *Landmark Briefs and Arguments*, 362–372.

p. 83, par. 4, Miller, "The Supreme Court As A Nation Builder."

p. 83, par. 4–5; p. 85, par. 1–3, Luther Martin, oral arguments, *McCulloch v. Maryland*, 4 Wheaton 316 (1819). Printed in *Landmark Briefs and Arguments*, 372–377.

p. 85, par. 6–p. 87, par. 5; p. 89, par. 2–p. 91, par. 4, William Pinkney, oral arguments, *McCulloch v. Maryland*, 4 Wheaton 316 (1819). Printed in *Landmark Briefs and Arguments*, 377–400.

p. 92, par. 2, William Draper Lewis, ed. *Great American Lawyers*, vol. 2. Philadelphia: The John C. Winston Company, 1907, 209.

p. 92, par. 2, Stephen M. Shapiro. "The Supreme Court's Greatest Advocate," Supreme Court and Appellate Practice Group Web site. http://www.appellate.net/articles/wilpin799.asp; also in Lewis, *Great American Lawyers*, 210–211.

Chapter 5

p. 93, par. 2, *McCulloch v. Maryland*, 4 Wheaton 316 (1819).

p. 102, par. 3, Stephen M. Shapiro, "The Supreme Court's

Greatest Advocate," Supreme Court and Appellate Practice Group Web site. http://www.appellate.net/ articles/wilpin799.asp

p. 102, par. 4, Robert H. Jackson, "Maryland at the Supreme Court," Maryland State Bar Association, 44 Md. S.B.A. Proc. III (1939).

Chapter 6

p. 103, par. 3, Robert H. Jackson, "Maryland at the Supreme Court," Maryland State Bar Association, 44 Md. S.B.A. Proc. III (1939).

p. 105, par. 1, *National Intelligencer* (March 13, 1819), cited in Jean Edward Smith, *John Marshall: Definer of a Nation*. New York: Owl Books, 1998, 446.

p. 105, par. 2, Joseph Story (March 7, 1819), cited in "The Federal Bar and the Law, 1815–1830," *The Informer*. http://www.atgpress.com/inform/abo13.htm

p. 105, par. 3, *National Intelligencer* (March 13, 1819), cited in Smith, *John Marshall*, 446.

p. 105, par. 4, Robert H. Jackson, "Maryland at the Supreme Court."

p. 105, par. 4, *Niles Register* (March 13, 1819), cited in "The Federal Bar and the Law, 1815–1830," *The Informer*. http://www.atgpress.com/inform/ abo13.htm

p. 105, par. 5, *Richmond Enquirer* (1819), cited in "The Federal Bar and the Law, 1815–1830," *The Informer*.

p. 106, par. 1, Supreme Court Historical Society, "The Marshall Court, 1801–1835," *History of the Court*. http://www.supremecourthistory.org/02_history/ subs_history/02_c04.html

p. 106, par. 1, Harvey H. Miller, "The Supreme Court As A Nation Builder," paper presented at American College of Bankruptcy Induction Ceremony, March 18, 2005.

p. 107, par. 1, William Story, ed., *Life and Letters of Joseph*

Story, vol. 1. Boston: Little and Brown, 1851, 411.

p. 108, par. 1, John Marshall, "Judicial Review, letter, 1823," S. Mintz (2003). *Digital History*. http://www.digitalhistory.uh.edu/documents/ documents_p2.cfm?doc=350

p. 108, par. 2, *Cohens* v. *Virginia*, 19 U.S. 264 (1821).

p. 109, par. 1, Paul Leicester Ford, "The Works of Thomas Jefferson, vol. 12 (Correspondence and Papers 1816–1826)." The Online Library of Liberty, 2005. http://oll.libertyfund.org/Home3/HTML.php ?recordID=0054.12

p. 111, par. 1, *Mistretta* v. *United States*, 488 U.S. 361 (1989).

p. 111, par. 2, "Enumerated, Implied, Resulting, and Inherent Powers," Annotations, 3. http://caselaw.lp.findlaw.com/data/constitution/ article01/03.html

p. 113, par. 1, Richard Kluger, *Simple Justice*. New York: Alfred A. Knopf, 1976, 600–601.

FurTHer InFormaTIon

Books

Ball, Lea. *The Federalist-Anti-Federalist Debate over States' Rights: A Primary Source Investigation*, Great Historic Debates and Speeches. New York: Rosen Publishing Group, 2004.

Banks, Joan. *The U.S. Constitution*, Your Government: How It Works. Broomall, PA.: Chelsea House Publications, 2001.

Barber, Benjamin R. *A Passion for Democracy*. Princeton, NJ: Princeton University Press, 2000.

Barber, Nathan. *Get Wise! Mastering U.S. History*. Lawrenceville, NJ: Peterson's Guides, 2004.

Bober, Natalie S. *Thomas Jefferson: Man on a Mountain*. New York: Simon Pulse, 1997.

Bradford, M. E. *Founding Fathers: Brief Lives of the Framers of the United States Constitution*. Lawrence: University Press of Kansas, 1994.

Brookhiser, Richard. *Alexander Hamilton, American*. New York: Free Press, 2000.

Cornelius, Kay. *The Supreme Court*, Your Government: How It Works. Broomall, PA.: Chelsea House Publications, 2000.

Hamilton, Alexander. *Opinion as to the Constitutionality of the Bank of the United States*. Kila, MT: Kessinger Publishing, 2004.

Heath, David, and Charlotte Wilcox. *The Supreme Court of the United States*, American Civics. Mankato, MN.: Bridgestone Books, 1999.

Heidler, David S. *Daily Life in the Early American Republic, 1790-1820: Creating a New Nation*, The Greenwood Press Daily Life Through History Series. Westport, CT: Greenwood Press, 2004.

Kaplan, Edward S. *The Bank of the United States and the American Economy*, Contributions in Economics and Economic History. Westport, CT: Greenwood Press, 1999.

National Archives. *Our Documents: 100 Milestone Documents from the National Archives*. New York: Oxford University Press, 2003.

Patrick, John J. *The Supreme Court of the United States: A Student Companion*, Oxford Student Companions to American Government, 2nd ed. New York: Oxford University Press Children's Books, 2002.

Sanders, Mark C. *Supreme Court*, American Government Today Series. Austin, TX: Raintree/Steck-Vaughn Publishers, 2001.

Smith, Jean Edward. *John Marshall: Definer Of A Nation*. New York: Henry Holt & Company, 1996.

Taylor, George Rogers. *Jackson versus Biddle: The Struggle Over the Second Bank of the United States*. Lexington, MA: D. C. Heath, 1967.

Webster, Daniel. Mr. Webster's Speeches in the Senate, upon the Question of Renewing the Charter of the Bank of the United States. Washington, D.C.: Printed by Gales and Seaton, (1832).

Videotapes/Audiotapes

Irons, Peter, ed. *May It Please the Court: Courts, Kids, and the Constitution*. New York: The New York Press, 2000. Live recordings and transcripts of the Supreme

Court oral arguments (audio).

Just The Facts—The United States Bill of Rights and Constitutional Amendments, Just the Facts series. Camarillo, CA: Goldhil Home Media I, 2004 (video).

Profiles of Freedom: A Living Bill of Rights. Arlington, VA: Bill of Rights Institute, 1997 (video).

Web Sites
Avalon Project at Yale Law School.
http://www.yale.edu/lawweb/avalon/amerdoc/bank-tj.htm
http://www.yale.edu/lawweb/avalon/18th.htm

Close Up Foundation.
http://www.closeup.org/federal.htm

FindLaw (U.S. Supreme Court Cases).
http://www.findlaw.com/casecode/supreme.html

FoundingFathers.info (*Federalist Papers*).
http://www.foundingfathers.info/federalistpapers/
hamilton.htm

From Revolution to Reconstruction—an .HTML project of the Department of Alfa-Informatica of the University of Groningen, The Netherlands.
http://www.let.rug.nl/usa/D/1801-1825/marshallcases/
mar05.htm

"JEC Legal Glossary," Judicial Education Center of New Mexico.
http://jec.unm.edu/resources/glossaries/
general-glossary.htm

Landmark Cases of the U.S. Supreme Court.
http://www.landmarkcases.org/mcculloch/home.html

Legal Information Institute, Cornell Law School.
http://www.law.cornell.edu

Library of Congress, American Memory section.
http://memory.loc.gov/ammem/collections/continental

National Archives, original documents.
http://www.archives.gov

Oyez Project: U.S. Supreme Court Multimedia Web site.
http://www.oyez.org/oyez/frontpage

Supreme Court of the United States.
http://www.supremecourtus.gov

Supreme Court Historical Society.
http://www.supremecourthistory.org

ThisNation.com. American Government & Politics
Online.
http://www.thisnation.com/federalism.html

TeachingAmericanHistory.org
http://teachingamericanhistory.org/convention

BIBLIOGRAPHY

Articles

Atkins, Chris. "Important Tax Cases: *McCullough* v. *Maryland* and the Sovereign Power to Tax." Tax Foundation Tax Policy Blog (August 10, 2005). http://www.taxfoundation.org/blog/show/1002.htm

Cowen, David. "The First Bank of the United States." EH.net Encyclopedia Web site. http://eh.net/encyclopedia/article/cowen.banking.first_bank.us

Dacor Bacon House Foundation, "The History of the Dacor Bacon House," Dacor Bacon House Foundation Web site. http://www.dacorbacon.org/DBHF/Dacor_Bacon_House.htm

Dixon, Richard. "John Marshall (1755–1835), *From Revolution to Reconstruction . . . and what happened afterwards, an .HTML project.* Groningen, The Netherlands: Department of Alfa-informatica, University of Groningen, 2001. http://odur.let.rug.nl/~usa/B/jmarshall/marsh.htm

FindLaw. "Enumerated, Implied, Resulting, and Inherent Powers," Annotations. Findlaw Web site. http://caselaw.lp.findlaw.com/data/constitution/article01/03.html

Informer, The. "The Federal Bar and the Law, 1815–1830," *The Informer.* http://www.atgpress.com/inform/abo13.htm

Ireland, Robert M. "William Pinkney: A Revision and Re-emphasis," *American Journal of Legal History* 14, no. 3 (July 1970).

Jackson, Robert H. "Maryland at the Supreme Court," Maryland State Bar Association, 44 Md. S.B.A. Proc. III (1939).

Jones, John Paul. "Gabriel Duvall," in the OYEZ Project, www.oyez.org/justices/justice/?justice=seat-six/gabriel_duvall

Klarman, Michael J., "How Great were the 'Great' Marshall Court Decisions?" *Virginia Law Review* 87, (October 2001) 1111-1184. Available online at SSRN: http://ssrn.com/abstract=279090

Kurland, Philip B., and Gerhard Casper, eds. *Landmark Briefs and Arguments of the Supreme Court of the United States: Constitutional Law*, Vol. 1. Washington, DC: University Publications of America Inc., 1978.

Lane, Calvin. "Joseph Story, Associate Justice, U.S. Supreme Court," Exploring Amistad at Mystic Seaport Web site. http://amistad.mysticseaport.org/discovery/people/bio.story.joseph.html

Lee, Rex E. "Remarks on the Bicentennial of the Supreme Court," *Supreme Court Historical Society 1990 Yearbook*, digital collection from the Supreme Court Historical Society. http://www.supremecourthistory.org/04_library/subs_volumes/04c_12_e.html

Library of Virginia, "John Marshall," an exhibition at the Library of Virginia (January 8, 2001–March 31, 2001). http://www.lva.lib.va.us/whoweare/exhibits/marshall/index.htm

Linder, Douglas O. "Justice Joseph Story," in *Famous American Trials: Amistad Trials*, University of Missouri School of Law Web site, 1998. http://www.law.umkc.edu/faculty/projects/ftrials/amistad/ami_bsto.htm

Luria, Sarah. "National Domesticity in the Early Republic: Washington, D.C.," *Common-Place* 3 (July 2003): 4. http://www.common-place.org/vol-03/no-04/washington

Miller, Harvey H. "The Supreme Court As A Nation Builder," paper presented at American College of Bankruptcy Induction Ceremony, March 18, 2005.

National Park Service. "First Bank of the United States," The U.S. Constitution. National Park Service Web site. http://www.cr.nps.gov/history/online_books/butowsky2/constitution5.htm

Packard, Joseph. "General Walter Jones," *Virginia Law Register* 7, no. 4 (August 1901).

Rehnquist, William H. "John Marshall." Remarks at the College of William and Mary, Williamsburg, VA, October 6, 2000. Available online from the U.S. Supreme Court Web site. http://www.supremecourtus.gov/publicinfo/speeches/sp_10-06-00.html

Robert, Joseph C. "The Many-Sided Attorney General," *Supreme Court Historical Society 1976 Yearbook*, digital collection from the Supreme Court Historical Society. http://www.supremecourthistory.org/04_library/subs_volumes/04_c01_g.html

Shapiro, Stephen M. "William Pinkney: The Supreme Court's Greatest Advocate." Appellate.net: Supreme Court and Appellate Practice Group Web site (1999). http://www.appellate.net/articles/wilpin799.asp

Supreme Court Historical Society. "The Marshall Court, 1801–1835," *History of the Court*. Supreme Court Historical Society Web site. http://www.supremecourthistory.org/02_history/subs_history/02_c04.html

U.S. Information Agency. "Reinventing American Federalism," *Issues of Democracy, Electronic Journal of the U.S. Information Agency* 2, no. 2 (April 1997).

White, G. Edward. "Imagining the Marshall Court,"

Supreme Court Historical Society 1986 Yearbook, digital collection from the Supreme Court Historical Society. http://www.supremecourthistory.org/04 _library/subs_volumes/04_c18_m.html

Books

Amber, Douglas G. *Cases & Materials on American Federalism*. Hammond, IN: Purdue University Calumet, 2006. http://www.agh-attorneys.com/ 3_camo _contents.htm

Barber, Benjamin R. *A Passion for Democracy*. Princeton, NJ: Princeton University Press, 2000.

Baxter, Maurice Glen. *Daniel Webster and the Supreme Court*. Amherst, MA: University of Massachusetts Press, 1966.

Boles, John B. *A Guide to the Microfilm Edition of the William Wirt Papers, 1784–1864*. Baltimore: Maryland Historical Society (1971).

Corwin, Edward S. *John Marshall and the Constitution*. The Library of American Freedoms. Richmond, IN: Palladium Press, 2004.

Hamilton, Alexander. *The Federalist Papers*, available online at University of Oklahoma College of Law Web site, http://www.law.ou.edu/hist/federalist/

_____. *The Works of Alexander Hamilton*, ed. Henry Cabot Lodge, 12 vols. Federal Edition, New York: G.P. Putnam's Sons, 1904. Available online at the Online Library of Liberty Web site. http://oll.libertyfund. org/Home3/Set.php?recordID=0249

_____. *The Works of Thomas Jefferson*, ed. Paul Leicester Ford. Vol. 12. Correspondence and Papers 1816–1826. New York: Knickerbocker, 1905. Available online at the Online Library of Liberty Web site. http://oll .libertyfund.org/Home3/Set.php?recordID=0249

Kennedy, John F. *Profiles in Courage*. New York: Harper Perennial Modern Classics, 2004.

Kluger, Richard. *Simple Justice*. New York: Alfred A. Knopf, 1976.

Lewis, William Draper, ed. *Great American Lawyers*. Vol. 2. Philadelphia: The John C. Winston Company, 1907.

Rossiter, Clinton. *Alexander Hamilton and the Constitution*. New York: Harcourt, Brace & World, Inc., 1964

Smith, Jean Edward. *John Marshall: Definer Of A Nation*. New York: Henry Holt & Company, 1996.

Story, William, ed. *Life and Letters of Joseph Story*. Vol. 1. Boston: Little and Brown, 1851.

Wright, Robert E. *Hamilton Unbound: Finance and the Creation of the American Republic*. Contributions in Economics and Economic History. Westport, CT: Praeger Publishers, 2002.

Cases/Documents

Brown v. *Board of Education*, 347 U.S. 483 (1954).

Cohens v. *Virginia*, 19 U.S. 264 (1821).

Dartmouth College v. *Woodward*, 17 U.S. 518 (1819).

Gibbons v. *Ogden*, 22 U.S. 1 (1824).

Hamilton, Alexander. "Hamilton's Opinion as to the Constitutionality of the Bank of the United States, 1791." The Avalon Project at Yale Law School. http://www.yale.edu/lawweb/avalon/amerdoc/bank-tj.htm

Jefferson, Thomas. "Jefferson's Opinion on the Constitutionality of a National Bank, 1791." The Avalon Project at Yale Law School. http://www.yale.edu/lawweb/avalon/amerdoc/bank-tj.htm

———. *Papers*. ME 6:388, Papers 12:440, available online at University of Virginia Library Web site. http://etext.virginia.edu/jefferson/texts

McCulloch v. *Maryland*. 4 Wheaton 316 (1819).

133

Marbury v. *Madison*, 5 U.S. 137 (1803).

Marshall, John. "Judicial Review, letter, 1823," S. Mintz (2003). *Digital History*. http://www.digitalhistory.uh .edu/documents/documents_p2.cfm?doc=350

Mistretta v. *United States*, 488 U.S. 361 (1989).

New York Times v. *United States*, 403 U.S. 713 (1971).

Sturges v. *Crowninshield*, 4 Wheaton 122 (1819).

U.S. Constitution.

Web Sites

Administrative Office of the U.S. Courts.
http://www.uscourts.gov

Avalon Project at Yale Law School.
http://www.yale.edu/lawweb/avalon/amerdoc/bank-tj.htm

Digital History, "Judicial Review."
http://www.digitalhistory.uh.edu/documents/
documents_p2.cfm?doc=350

FindLaw (U.S. Supreme Court Cases).
http://www.findlaw.com/casecode/supreme.html

From Revolution to Reconstruction—an .HTML project of
the Department of Alfa-Informatica of the University
of Groningen, The Netherlands.
http://www.let.rug.nl/usa/D/1801-1825/marshall cases/
mar05.htm

Iowa Court Information System.
http://www.judicial.state.ia.us/

"JEC Legal Glossary," Judicial Education Center of New
Mexico. http://jec.unm.edu/resources/glossaries/
general-glossary.htm

Landmark Cases of the U.S. Supreme Court.
http://www.landmarkcases.org/mcculloch/home.html

Legal Information Institute, Cornell Law School.
http://www.law.cornell.edu

Oyez Project: U.S. Supreme Court Multimedia Web site.
http://www.oyez.org/oyez/frontpage

Pennsylvania Avenue National Historic Park Web site.
http://www.nps.gov/paav/hotels.htm

Supreme Court of the United States.
http://www.supremecourtus.gov

Supreme Court Historical Society.
http://www.supremecourthistory.org

U.S. Constitution Online.
http://www.usconstitution.net/consttop_fedr.html

index

Page numbers in **boldface** are illustrations, tables, and charts.

ABOUT THE AUTHOR

SUSAN DUDLEY GOLD has worked as a reporter for a daily newspaper, managing editor of two statewide business magazines, and freelance writer for several regional publications. She has written more than three dozen books for middle-school and high-school students on a variety of topics, including American history, health issues, law, and space.

Gold's *The Panama Canal Transfer: Controversy at the Crossroads* won first place in the nonfiction juvenile book category in the National Federation of Press Women's communications contest. Her book, *Sickle Cell Disease*, was named Best Book (science) by the Society of School Librarians International, as well as earning placement on Appraisal's top ten "Best Books" list. The American Association for the Advancement of Science honored another of her books, *Asthma*, as one of its "Best Books for Children." She has written several titles in the Supreme Court Milestones series for Marshall Cavendish.

In 2001 Gold received a Jefferson Award for community service in recognition of her work with a support group for people with chronic pain, which she founded in 1993. She and her husband, John Gold, own and operate a Web design and publishing business in Maine. They have one son, Samuel.